"I have personally known Jar
is family to me, my wife and m., —
tentional passionate pursuit of the Lord Jesus Christ. He has
spent his life seeking the face and heart of God and is a lover of
the Holy Spirit. He is an integrous model of a true prophet. I
highly recommend *The Lifestyle of a Prophet*, for its pages are
filled with insight, wisdom, revelation and the love of God."

> Dr. Ché Ahn, senior pastor of HRock Church, Pasadena,
> California; president of Harvest International Ministry;
> international chancellor of Wagner Leadership Institute

"This is not just a book for prophets or about prophets. It is a
relevant book of basics for every believer. Though James Goll is
a recognized prophet, he speaks to us all with pearls of wisdom
on every page. I know that you will love this book!"

> C. Peter Wagner, vice president of Global Spheres, Inc.

"James Goll is one of the most erudite scholars and voices in
the prophetic arena in the 21st-century Church. His journey
itself is a metaphor and parable of the call, the commissioning
and the crisis of prophetic ministry. The life and lifestyle of the
prophet is the foundation for all that a prophet speaks and does.
James is a man of honor, integrity and authority in the Spirit.
This latest work is the culmination of his journey thus far and a
must-have for anyone desirous of understanding and cooperat-
ing with heaven in order to realize a recovery of the testimony
of Jesus (which is the spirit of prophecy) in this generation."

> Dr. Mark J. Chironna, founder and senior pastor of Church
> On The Living Edge, Orlando, Florida; Mark Chironna
> Ministries

"James Goll's powerful book *The Lifestyle of a Prophet* is more
than a book. It is a field-training manual for multitudes of people
who find themselves awakened to new spiritual dimensions and

yet struggle to navigate the whitewater of the prophetic gifting. Jim's book is full of fatherly insights and godly wisdom on how to live in intimacy, wisdom and revelation. *The Lifestyle of a Prophet* will inspire you to embrace your calling and become more like Jesus. I highly recommend this book!"

Kris Vallotton, senior associate leader of Bethel Church, Redding, California; co-founder of Bethel School of Supernatural Ministry; author of nine books, including *The Supernatural Ways of Royalty* and *Spirit Wars*

"*The Lifestyle of a Prophet* is not just for prophets or prophetically inclined individuals. It is a Holy Spirit–inspired devotional and teaching resource that should be on every believer's bookshelf. I love this book. I am confident that you will too!"

Patricia King, founder of XP Ministries

"This is an inspiring and challenging read! From nearly forty years of prophetic ministry experience, James Goll shares the wisdom and life lessons he has learned in his prophetic journey. James is a father in the faith with a heart to impart and raise up a legacy in the next generation. He has been a spiritual father and mentor to me personally. His balance between the Spirit and the Word make his insights invaluable. As you read this book, you will learn not only deep lessons of what it is to be called and prepared as a prophetic voice, but also how to live a prophetic lifestyle and walk in the fullness of your own calling and destiny. James brings a great mix of personal life experience with solid biblical revelation. Not only will you be inspired, but you will also be instructed in how to live an authentic prophetic life like Jesus and others in the Bible. Get ready to glean from a true father in the prophetic."

Matt Sorger, head of Matt Sorger Ministries

The Lifestyle of a Prophet

The Lifestyle

OF A

Prophet

A 21-DAY JOURNEY TO EMBRACING YOUR CALLING

JAMES W. GOLL

FOREWORD BY JOHN LOREN SANDFORD

Chosen

a division of Baker Publishing Group
Minneapolis, Minnesota

© 2001, 2013 by James W. Goll

Previously published under the title *The Coming Prophetic Revolution*

Published by Chosen Books
11400 Hampshire Avenue South
Bloomington, Minnesota 55438
www.chosenbooks.com

Chosen Books is a division of
Baker Publishing Group, Grand Rapids, Michigan

Printed in the United States of America

Library of Congress Cataloging-in-Publication Data
Goll, Jim W.
    The lifestyle of a prophet : a 21-day journey to embracing your calling / James W. Goll ; foreword by John Loren Sandford.
    p. cm.
    Includes bibliographical references.
    Summary: "This unique, hands-on 21-day guide helps all believers develop intimacy with God so they can hear his voice clearly—and then proclaim his words faithfully"—Provided by publisher.
    ISBN 978-0-8007-9536-8 (pbk. : alk. paper)
    1. Spirituality. 2. Spiritual life—Christianity. I. Title.
    BV4501.3.G6565 2013
    248.4—dc23
                                            2012042339

Cover design by Lookout Design, Inc.

The internet addresses, email addresses, and phone numbers in this book are accurate at the time of publication. They are provided as a resource. Baker Publishing Group does not endorse them or vouch for their content or permanence.

17   18   19   20   10 9 8 7 6

Dedication and Acknowledgments

This book is dedicated to my four miracle children, now all grown adults—Justin, GraceAnn, Tyler and Rachel. This book is about something that is coming—something on the horizon, something not yet fully here. You will see; it will be your generation, and perhaps the generation after you, that will fully come into the contents written in this devotional book of yearnings. My prayer is that you will be right in the middle of the greatest authentic move of God that has ever hit Planet Earth.

Thank you guys for sharing and releasing me to the nations over the many years and believing in your good old dad. You have sacrificed so very much. Thank you for your prayers and patience with me. You make my heart glad. May you each be the unique vessel that God has created you to be. May you carry the generational prophetic anointing to impact the cultural mountain God and you choose together. I love each one of you so very much! You are each amazing!

And as your dear mom used to say, "I'm gonna take that mountain!" She was always so trusting and tenacious. So follow in her footsteps and always believe—"Ain't no mountain high enough—to keep me from You!" And that You, of course, is all about our passionate pursuit of the God who first loved us and has proved Himself over and over again that He alone is more than enough!

I also wish to thank the editorial and marketing team of Chosen Books with which I have had the honor of working for the past fifteen years. I thank the Lord for my excellent assistant, David Sluka, who has helped me take the original manuscript and shift it into this format. I thank the Lord for all the mentors over the years who have poured into my life so that I could bring forth equipping materials to further God's prophetic purposes throughout the earth.

With joy, I dedicate this book of devotion to my four kids.

Your Cheerleading Dad

Contents

Contents

Foreword

James Goll has written a magnificent book. Many prophetic books may overflow our personal libraries—most good but few deserving to become classics, valuable for each succeeding generation. I hope *The Lifestyle of a Prophet* comes to be regarded as such. It deserves it.

The first section, "The Lifestyle of Intimacy," calls all who would serve God in the office of the prophetic into a discipline of daily intimacy. Few have stressed this area as much as it should have been stressed. We prophetic types sometimes become lax. But I can confirm James' word that only if we are walking close to our Lord moment by moment can we trust that what we think we are hearing from God, and what we think we are being called to speak, really is from Him. There is a vast difference between a word from God and a word of God. Many may take what we say as a word from God, but it is of God only if we have, through intimacy, allowed Him to speak what He wants to speak through us.

The second section, "The Lifestyle of Wisdom," is well worth the purchase of the book. The list of advice in "Reading for Day 10" ought to be required not only for new prophetic types but for older prophets like me who need to be reminded of what we have known and too much forgotten. Those who feel called to present God's words—wherever and to whomever—would do well to refresh their minds in the wisdom of Day 11, "The Anatomy of a Prophetic Word." The fences of wisdom in this chapter are urgently needed to corral the wild horses of most prophets' sensitivities and imaginations before we speak what may not be of or even from God, as He and we would want.

There is balance and corporateness in what James Goll has written in the remaining days of Section 2 and in the final section, "The Lifestyle of Revelation." Keep *The Lifestyle of a Prophet* handy, to refer to as a doctor uses a manual to check proper vitamins and doses. No one can remember all the dos and don'ts stated wisely in this book. It will, therefore, be a handy and invaluable reference.

Those of us long weathered in the serene days and stormy seasons of the prophetic can resonate with James' statement in "The Anatomy of a Prophetic Word":

The ultimate goal of the prophetic is to reveal Christ. So the lifestyle of a prophet or those who walk in the prophetic should pull back the veil that the god of this age has put on the minds of unbelievers so they cannot see the light of the Gospel of the glory of Jesus Christ (see 2 Corinthians 4:3–4). When these wisdom parameters are in place, they will create a safe atmosphere where we can walk into fruitful prophetic maturation and faith can move freely.

John Loren Sandford, bestselling author; co-founder, Elijah House

Introduction

"Where do I begin to tell the story of . . . ?" A famous love song started out with these words many years ago. I am left in such a position as I ponder taking what has already been sixty-plus years of life and close to forty years of full-time vocational ministry and boiling it down into an inspirational devotional seasoned with sound teaching that will be an aid and not a boring, heavy exposition.

My book *The Coming Prophetic Revolution* (Chosen, 2001), was a meaty treatise written a bit ahead of its time. Though one of the most complete and thorough books I have ever written, it also was one of the most overlooked manuscripts that sat there on the shelf, per se. Forerunners can suffer from running too far ahead of the pack at times—though to them, they are right on track.

So we felt the need to revisit, update and shift the rich content within the original book. The outcome is *The Lifestyle of a Prophet*—a prophetic teaching and equipping devotional with readings for 21 days to help you embrace the prophetic calling of God on your life.

But how did I get started on my prophetic journey?

There are always those who go before you. For me it was primarily the prayers of my mother and the devotion of my late wife, Michal Ann. They are some of my heroes and belong in my modern Hall of Fame and the great cloud of witnesses that surround us today. There have been many other positive influences as well in my journey of developing a prophetic lifestyle.

Then there was the solidity of the teachers of the charismatic renewal—the crazy infectious zeal of the Jesus People culture mingled with the impact of the integrity of the Third Wave movement. Then I rode the tidal wave that hit the shores of the Body of Christ in the prophetic movement and the role I played in those formative years in Kansas City. This, of course, has been followed by the apostolic reformation, which in my perspective is still in its formation. All of these movements and their various leaders have impacted me greatly. I have been exposed to many lessons about what to do and what not to repeat. Someday, when I am older, I want to compose a book entitled *Lessons from the Woodshed*! But that is for another day.

None of these great movements or trailblazers and forerunners ever takes the place of cultivating your very own personal walk and talk with the Holy Spirit by your side. He personally directs you to be more like Jesus by teaching us through life's journey that God the Father is good all the time. Whew, that says a lot! Yep, you heard me. One of the biggest lessons New Testament prophets today must learn and exhibit is that God is good—period. Now that is a revelation worth living! I have already seen a lot of good fruit and, well, I have also seen some things I personally do not want to see repeated. Many of the lessons I have learned along the way are contained in this book.

So whom is this book for? With the title *Lifestyle of a Prophet*, I want to make it clear that this book is not just about the making of a prophet or even just a great company of prophetic ministers. It is first and foremost about being a disciple of the

Lord Jesus Christ—following in the lifestyle of One who did only what He saw the Father doing and said only what He heard the Father saying (see John 5:19; 8:28). If your heart says, "Not my will, but Yours be done," you will receive much as you read the following pages.

Obviously I believe that prophets are for today, but part of their role is to raise up a community of believers who live a prophetic lifestyle. I will let you read the book for yourself and learn some lessons from one who has walked this journey all his life.

You will notice I have divided the lifestyle journey into three sections: "The Lifestyle of Intimacy," "The Lifestyle of Wisdom" and "The Lifestyle of Revelation." Please make note of the order. Many people make the mistake of promoting the prophetic lifestyle first and foremost as being about pursuing higher-level gifts. From my vantage point, that is a recipe for disaster.

So let's dive right in and cultivate a lifestyle of intimacy, wisdom and revelation. Maybe this book will help you discover your own personal calling in God. I sure hope so! After all, it is not just a few good prophets the Holy Spirit desires. He longs for an entire prophetic generation to arise that loves truth and is centered in the character of Jesus and releases the fragrance of Christ into every facet of society. After all, a true prophet does not point to oneself, but to the One. He alone is worthy. He alone is the reason I live.

May you be blessed!

Dr. James W. Goll, Encounters Network

The Lifestyle of Intimacy

"I have made Your name known to them, and will make it known to them, so that the love with which You love Me may be in them, and I in them."

JOHN 17:26

John—Prophet of Beloved Intimacy

"There is a friend who sticks closer than a brother," says Proverbs 18:24. Jesus did not have too many of those friends during His greatest hour of need. Did you realize that John was the only disciple of the Twelve specifically named as having been at Jesus' crucifixion? We know Simon of Cyrene helped to carry His cross, and that a group of women followers of the Messiah were present (see Luke 23:26–27). It is also well documented that Mary, the mother of Jesus, was looking on, accompanied by her sister, Mary the wife of Clopas, and Mary Magdalene (see John 19:25). I wonder where the others were.

But John, the beloved, the friend of Jesus, was there. No wonder he speaks so much in his writings about the love and forgiveness of God and was the only disciple to record the words of Jesus, "Greater love has no one than this, that one lay down his life for his friends" (John 15:13). This John actually saw the crucifixion. He witnessed the effects of the crown of thorns piercing the brow of the Savior. He saw the face of Jesus marred. He saw the results of the 39 lashes on His lacerated, raw back. John witnessed firsthand the nails piercing His hands and feet. He heard the desperate cries of the Son of Man, the only Son of God, for help. The sound of Jesus' words from the cross probably echoed in John's heart and mind all his life.

According to John 21:20, the John who was at the cross was the same John who had laid his head on the chest of the Messiah at the Last Supper. I wonder what all he heard when his ear was so close to Jesus?

John's journey with his Lord took a different turn from that of the others. He laid his head on the chest of the Creator of the universe. He saw the excruciating ordeal of the criminal death of an innocent Man. He was also given an amazing stewardship—the ongoing care of Jesus' mother, Mary (see John 19:27). I would give over the care of my mother only into the very best hands.

I wonder what Jesus saw in John. What was different in him? Did he have an uncommon love for his Master?

Later in life this same disciple spoke of simple things. He groomed the next generation, and generations to come, whetting their appetites by penning his epistles with words of love. I wonder why.

Let's pause for a moment. Why bring up the apostle John in a book entitled *The Lifestyle of a Prophet*? You would probably expect another John—John the Baptist—or an Old Testament prophet like Elijah, Isaiah or Daniel. Why John the Beloved?

I begin with John because the lifestyle of a prophet must begin with love. No one's life or writings better exemplify a lifestyle of love and intimacy than that of John. I believe that it was from that place that John also received and delivered a prophetic revelation the Church anticipates to this day: the Second Coming of King Jesus. We must remember that keys like intimacy, devotion, faithfulness and friendship with God are how you embrace the One who calls you and ultimately discover your calling. So let's look more closely at the life of John, the beloved disciple, to find some keys to a lifestyle of intimacy.

John's Radical Surrender

In the following Scripture we see the cost of enlisting in a revolutionary army.

> Going on from there He saw two other brothers, James the son of Zebedee, and John his brother, in the boat with Zebedee their father, mending their nets; and He called them. Immediately they left the boat and their father, and followed Him.
>
> Matthew 4:21–22

John, who was transformed into a passionate lover of God, had lost everything he knew in order to come into that which he did not yet know. Oh, the cost of authentic discipleship! Now muse with me for a while. . . .

Zebedee was raising his family to be God-fearers. Like other good fathers, he was also teaching his sons a trade that they, too, would be expected to pass on to their sons. Zebedee, a Jewish man, had probably studied the Torah and the prophets and had been taught that one day the Messiah would come. He would also have read in Isaiah that there would come a forerunner calling for every crooked way to be made straight.

Then some strange man wearing a coat of camel's hair emerged from the wilderness. He had a peculiar diet and an even stranger demeanor. Word was already circulating for the Jews to be leery of this on-the-fringes prophet called John the Baptist who was paving and pointing the way toward another whom he said was greater than he. He was preparing the way, so the Baptist said, for the Messiah. The whole region was in an uproar. Zebedee probably felt he needed to steady the boat a bit as people were getting into a frenzy.

Then the old man's worst dream came true. The One the prophet was pointing toward came and pointed His finger at Zebedee's heart. Jesus was on a pilgrimage to pick His own group of men to disciple. Sure enough, the young thirty-year-old appeared on the Galilean shores, came straight toward Zebedee's boat and did not even ask permission to speak to his two sons. Bypassing authority, the young zealot spoke right to the hearts of the young men: "Follow Me, and I will make you fishers of men" (Matthew 4:19). Immediately James and John jumped from the boat, left their father and started off on a new trek—the process of becoming a disciple.

Do you realize the cost they paid when they surrendered to their new Lord? No money, no job, no understandable future. They had just hurt the one person they had been trained all their lives to honor and whom they never wanted to bruise—their father. They left him to finish the fishing. They left him with no inheritance. But something in their hearts said, "Go." So they left all they knew to become something that their minds could not comprehend.

James and John understood fishing for fish. But what was fishing for men? What kind of bait do you use to do that? Sounds like a setup for a wrong interpretation of words of revelation, for misunderstanding what the Nazarene was really saying. Do you think there was the potential for false expectations?

Nonetheless off they went. And off went John in radical surrender to join an emerging new army of radical men who would jostle for position and misinterpret the sayings of their Leader. Mercy! Think John ever wanted to turn back and go home? I imagine so. But when you have been exposed to the real thing, there is no turning back.

So it is today with the emerging prophetic army our Lord is calling forth. Jesus said that no one can put his hand to the plow and look back (see Luke 9:62). You must keep looking forward. That is what John did. That is what you must do as well. Get ready to jump out of your comfortable boat. Make a radical surrender and become a catcher of men!

The Broken Vessel

Have you ever been scorched by the hot words of Jesus? Has He ever spoken something so deep into your heart that you were cut to the very core of your being? I think this is exactly what happened to John in the passage below. I believe he was pierced by God in his fleshly strength, never to recover.

> When His disciples James and John saw this, they said, "Lord, do You want us to command fire to come down from heaven and consume them?" But He turned and rebuked them.
>
> Luke 9:54–55

John started out like most of the rest of us—zealous, jealous and on hot fire. But along the way he became a broken vessel in the Lord's hands. Remember, through the culture of grace, disciples are made, not born. This John had made a radical surrender to his new Commander-in-Chief. Imagine having to learn new ways, a new vocation, hanging out with a bunch of men day and night, and following some itinerant around the country. Yeah, it would be exciting for a while. But when you get a prophetic word like, "You don't know what spirit you are speaking from!" that might set you back for a while.

Realize that most of these new followers were probably just in their early twenties. John and James were even named *Boanerges* by the Lord, which means "Sons of Thunder" (Mark 3:17). After they had followed Jesus for almost three years, they were still jostling for position, and their mother, Salome, was even stirring them up to do it. They were contending to see which one could sit on Jesus' right hand and which on His left (see Mark 10:35–41). Sounds as if John and his brother had more zeal than wisdom. Does that sound familiar?

But every "son of thunder" needs the wisdom of a father to help nurture and love him into all God has created him to be.

Did you ever have more zeal than knowledge of God's ways? Ever get in His way instead of out of it? Ever have the wrong concept of what prophetic ministry looks like, and you just wanted to call down fire on everyone? After all, you are called to be a prophet of judgment, and you know God has chosen you to call it down. (And in your opinion, sooner would be better than later!)

Maybe mercy needs to triumph in your life, as it did in John's. We need prophets who love mercy and who want to call *that* kind of fire down on people, cities and nations. Judgmental, prophetic lone rangers do not last long; team ministry is the higher pathway. Are you in this for the long haul or just the short run? To judge a city or build one up?

Yes, there are valleys to avoid and wisdom to be gained. There are valuable lessons to grasp, like the fact that selfish ambition is not the Kingdom way. Promotion does come from the Lord, but normally after you have been in the game and endured a few rounds. John became a broken vessel, and it was pleasing to the Lord. See him—and yourself—yielded, merciful and leaning on the Master's chest.

John's Testimony of Jesus

As an aged man, John was exiled in solitude on the Isle of Patmos. He seems to have nothing left in his life. He is abandoned by men—but not by God. Not at all by God and His brilliant presence! God is now his constant companion.

> I fell at his feet to worship him. But he said to me, "Do not do that; I am a fellow servant of yours and your brethren who hold the testimony of Jesus; worship God. For the testimony of Jesus is the spirit of prophecy."
>
> Revelation 19:10

First John 1:1 wonderfully states, "What was from the beginning, what we have heard, what we have seen with our eyes, what we have looked at and touched with our hands, concerning the Word of Life. . . ." Is this the same man? How did this transformation take place? The motivation seems different; the focus of the message is distinctly changed. This man is not talking about calling down judgment. He is not just teaching about gifts and ministries. He is speaking about a life consumed by the Person of God Himself.

In the midst of all this, he gives us a revolutionary concept concerning the central issue of what authentic prophetic ministry is all about: *Worship God!* Worship God, and you will be walking in the opposite spirit from that of this world. And as you worship God, someone—the great Someone—will inhabit your praises, and the Holy Spirit's revelatory presence will be poured out. Yes, the true heart of the prophet is the testimony not of how great you are, but of how awesome He is! The testimony of Jesus is the spirit of prophecy.

Do you want to become a true messenger of the Lord with fire burning in your bones? Then have the Man of fire dwelling in your heart. Abandon any attempts to build your own kingdom or ministry. Forget about building your own empire; build His instead. Worship God passionately. Consecrate yourself to Him to be His holy dwelling place.

John, the "Son of Thunder," was changed. John the fisherman became a wisdom spout for the purposes of God. He taught people how to forgive, how to love, how to cover one another. In fact, his last writing is not as much a scenario of end-times cataclysmic things as it is a profound epistle concerning the revelation of Jesus Christ Himself.

Do you want to experience the lifestyle of a prophet? It begins with intimacy. Surrender to Jesus and worship Him.

The next six readings are focused around aspects of a lifestyle of intimacy. At the end of each reading is a devotional section to help you process what you have read and embrace its application for your life.

The book of John records the following prayer of Jesus spoken to His Father on the night of His betrayal. He asked that "the love with which You loved Me may be in them, and I in them" (John 17:26). What a glorious, intimate love that is! Jesus is longing to be your intimate Friend. Will you be His?

⟩ P R A Y E R ⟨

Father, I present myself to You right now. I surrender to Jesus as my Lord and Savior, and also as my Friend. I lay down my life before You and ask that You would pick it up and lead me on Your paths for Your name's sake. Heal my brokenness and make me whole. Thank You that You do not just tolerate me, You love me and delight in who I am. As I read the words of this book, breathe upon me and draw me close to encounter You. Like John, I desire to walk in intimacy with You. Come, Lord, and embrace me. Lead me into a more intimate lifestyle of love. I love You and want to love You more. Take me on this journey to be more like You. For Jesus' sake, Amen.

⋙Embracing Your Calling—Day 1

1. Consider the kind of friendship you desire to have with Jesus. What do you want that relationship to look like?

2. What comforts have you surrendered to follow Jesus?

3. How has God produced brokenness in your life so that you can live with passion but also with wisdom?

4. Take a few moments right now to worship Jesus. Thank Him for His goodness in your life. Be specific. Then tell Jesus of your desire to live a lifestyle of intimacy with God.

The Intimate Breath of God

A battle is being waged in our day—an end-time battle of passions, an unprecedented competition between the altars of fire. The spirit of this world is out of control and vying for the attention of any half-interested soul. Sometimes it seems we have more "Hollywood" than "holy good" in the Church.

But good news is on the horizon. This fierce fight of the ages will escalate as waves of God's irresistible love wash over us and the constraints of stale religiosity are replaced by passionate, fiery, relatable Christianity. A revolution of intimacy is coming in the Church. Is that not what your heart is aching for? Like John, the beloved disciple of Jesus, we, too, shall learn to lean our heads on our Master's chest and rest in the sound of His heart beating in the rhythm of love (see John 21:20).

As we look at the lifestyle of intimacy in the life of a prophet, let me share with you some thoughts and principles drawn from the book of Genesis on the relationship between intimacy and the prophetic.

Genesis 2:7 grants some awesome relational insights: "The LORD God formed man of dust from the ground, and breathed into his nostrils the breath of life; and man became a living being." What a beginning! All humankind took on life by the very breath of God's mouth. Talk about an intimate exchange! Ponder this for a while. In some manner God blew into the lump of clay that He had fashioned, and Adam's body took on an added dimension. Man became a living being.

That is what the prophetic life and ministry are all about—human beings being filled with the breath of God, and then in turn exhaling onto others the breath of life they have received from their Creator. This is what our Messiah did as well. After His resurrection He appeared to His disciples, who were hiding for fear. He said, "As the Father has sent Me, I also send you" (John 20:21). Then Jesus breathed on them and said, "Receive the Holy Spirit" (verse 22).

At the Last Supper of Jesus with His trainees, John leaned back on the Lord's chest (see John 13:25). What do you think he heard? Yes, probably the pulsating heart of the Savior, but he also would have heard something else: the Messiah's very breath as He inhaled and exhaled. Imagine being so close to the Lord that you hear Him breathing!

Some of the writers of the past knew something of this intimacy. Consider the hymn "Breathe on Me, Breath of God" written in 1878 by Edwin Hatch:

> Breathe on me, Breath of God,
> Fill me with life anew,
> That I may love what Thou dost love,
> And do what Thou wouldst do.
>
> Breathe on me, Breath of God,
> Until my heart is pure,
> Until with Thee I will one will,
> To do and to endure.
>
> Breathe on me, Breath of God,
> Till I am wholly Thine,

Till all this earthly part of me
Glows with Thy fire divine.

Breathe on me, Breath of God,
So shall I never die,
But live with Thee the perfect life
Of Thine eternity.

Yes, man became a living being when the intimate breath of almighty God was blown into Adam's lungs. So it was that he became a transporter of God's presence, a contagious carrier of the infectious Spirit of God.

God's Original Design

God's original intent was for all of us to be carriers of His presence. Today the Lord is looking for vessels He can breathe into once again. He seeks some that He can put His mouth upon, as it were, and blow His Spirit into them, so that their lungs, their hearts, their souls, their bodies, their temples will be filled with the very breath of the Almighty. He wants us to be carriers of His most brilliant presence. What could be greater?

That was the Lord's original intent. And we know what followed: "For this reason a man shall leave his father and his mother, and be joined to his wife; and they shall become one flesh. And the man and his wife were both naked and were not ashamed" (Genesis 2:24–25). Here we are given a graphic picture of what things look like when a man or woman is filled with the brilliance of God's presence. When we are filled with His *pneuma* (the Greek word for *breath*), we are not self-absorbed and fearful but walking with God and others in transparent love.

Adam and Eve were not ashamed. They were not overcome by guilt, nor were they driven by condemnation. They were not hiding behind whatever leaves they could find. They were naked;

they were walking in honesty; they were enjoying intimate communion with God; and they "knew" each other.

That is God's design for marriage, which is the picture of the union He plans for us as the Bride of Jesus Christ (see Ephesians 5:22–32), our incredible, glorious Husband. This Master of ours wins our hearts with one glance of His eye (see Song of Solomon 4:9). And the amazing thing is, one glance of our own eyes shining back into His undoes His heart as well. What a profound mystery! The revelation of this truth alone would create a revolution of intimacy among God's people. It is awesome, and it is pictured right here in the Garden of Eden, at the beginning of all things.

Adam and Eve were hiding behind nothing. Their hearts were beating with love for one another, and they were not ashamed. There were no barriers to intimacy.

The Problem

Look at what happened:

> [The serpent] said to the woman, "Indeed, has God said, 'You shall not eat from any tree of the garden'?" The woman said to the serpent, "From the fruit of the trees of the garden we may eat; but from the fruit of the tree which is in the middle of the garden, God has said, 'You shall not eat from it or touch it, or you will die.'"
>
> Genesis 3:1–3

God did not say they could not touch it—rather, that they could not eat it. So we see the enemy's tactic of exaggeration beginning already.

> The serpent said to the woman, "You surely will not die! For God knows that in the day you eat from it your eyes will be opened, and you will be like God, knowing good and evil." When the

31

woman saw that the tree was good for food, and that it was a delight to the eyes, and that the tree was desirable to make one wise, she took from its fruit and ate; and she gave also to her husband with her, and he ate. Then the eyes of both of them were opened, and they knew that they were naked; and they sewed fig leaves together and made themselves loin coverings.

Genesis 3:4–7

The deceiver acted out of his nature. Eve and Adam were deceived. Thus did sin and a cover-up plan come into being. Deception entered the world. Enticement drew the man and woman away from fellowship with their Maker. How I wonder what the heart of God felt at that moment! The crown of His creation had now rejected their Creator for a bit of false knowledge from a forbidden piece of fruit. How that must have grieved Him!

Previously all Adam and Eve had known was communion with God and with each other. All they had experienced was intimacy—relational love without fear of rejection. They would hear the Lord walking in the Garden (see Genesis 3:10) and walk and talk with Him. How marvelous! This is what they were created for—to commune with their Creator.

In the Garden with Our Beloved

In the little country Methodist church in the heartland where I grew up, we sang a marvelous hymn that shaped the course of my life, "I Come to the Garden Alone" by C. Austin Miles in 1912. This song, along with a few others, marked my heart at an early age for life.

> I come to the garden alone,
> While the dew is still on the roses;
> And the voice I hear, falling on my ear;
> The Son of God discloses.

[Refrain]
And He walks with me, and He talks with me,
And He tells me I am His own,
And the joy we share as we tarry there,
None other has ever known.

He speaks, and the sound of His voice
Is so sweet the birds hush their singing,
And the melody that He gave to me,
Within my heart is ringing.

I'd stay in the garden with Him
Tho' the night around me be falling,
But He bids me go; thru the voice of woe,
His voice to me is calling.

This old hymn depicts a beautiful communal relationship with our Beloved. That is the way it was in the beginning. But instead of "I come to the garden alone," God came into the Garden seeking fellowship with humankind. Imagine: They could actually hear Him walking! I wonder what the sound of God's footsteps sounded like.

I constantly ask God questions like this. I say, "Lord, what did that sound like? What was it like to hear You walking in the Garden? What did it sound like to hear Your voice on the wind?" I believe His walking with Adam and Eve in the Garden is not some old story in a dusty, antiquated book from yesteryear. It is reality.

God walks with me and He talks with me. This is what I was created for. And it is what *you* were made for, too—to walk and talk with our Master in the garden of His love. This is intimacy. If you and I would radically return to the arms of His intimate love, I am convinced there would be a prophetic revolution across the Body of Christ, and we would be awakened by the kisses of His love (see Song of Solomon 1:2).

With the right set of lenses on, you can see that this is all about a living relationship. Hearing God. Seeing God. Following

His lead. Sniffing out His trail. If only I could hear the echo of His footsteps. . . .

That is the heart of the prophetic. We are called to be a prophetic generation, a prophetic Church, a people leaning against Jesus with His heart pounding in our ears. Intimacy is the convergence of two hearts, His and ours, coming into rhythm together, so that there is only one sound. The writers of old, the desert fathers and the Christian mystics called this "greater union with Christ." Today, once again, the Lord is breathing these themes into life.

The Four Big Questions

Here were Adam and Eve, in transparent honesty and intimate communion with God. All of a sudden—uh-oh! Things changed. With their dignified coverings in place, Adam and Eve started playing hide-and-seek with God. When the Creator of the universe came on His daily stroll, they heard the familiar sound they had previously cherished. Then the Lord God called to them, "Where are you?" (Genesis 3:9).

Did He who has a commanding view of all things suddenly get spiritual amnesia and misplace the crown of His creation? Had He forgotten their names or blanked out on their address? What was He doing? Did the omnipotent and omniscient One not already know the answer?

Of course. But that was just one of four big questions the Lord asked of Adam and Eve—and He asks these questions of you and me—as they hid behind the barriers of shame, guilt and fear. Let's list the questions with their corresponding answers:

Question #1: "Where are you?"

Response: "I heard the sound of You in the garden, and I was afraid because I was naked; so I hid myself."

Questions #2 and #3: "Who told you that you were naked? Have you eaten from the tree of which I commanded you not to eat?"

Response: "The woman whom You gave to be with me, she gave me from the tree, and I ate."

Question #4: "What is this you have done?"

Response: "The serpent deceived me, and I ate."

Listen to these penetrating words:

"Where are you?"

"Who told you?"

"Have you eaten?"

"What is this you have done?"

Why did God ask these questions? Ponder for a moment and reflect on those times in your own life when the voice of God has asked *you* a question. Why does He do this? Here's the amazing truth: *Every question God asks is an invitation to intimacy!* Questions are an invitation into dialogue, to communion, to "come now, and let us reason together" (Isaiah 1:18).

God wants to talk to you. He wants more than just the "right" answers so you can pass His tests. He wants to draw near to you. He is your adoring Father and He cherishes His kids! Questions from the Lord are an invitation to emerge from the place of hiding into transparent honesty and light.

⟩ P R A Y E R ⟨

Father, Your original intent was that we would walk with You in a place of intimacy. I desperately desire to have a lifestyle of intimacy in my walk with You—walking with You, talking with You, ministering to others with

You fully alive in me and expressing Yourself through me. Speak to me. Your servant is listening. I long to be a carrier of Your glorious presence—spreading the fragrance of Your likeness everywhere I go. Continue to come upon me with waves of Your presence until I become all that You have for me to be. Let waves of Your great love flood me now and the wind of Your Spirit blow across my life. Draw me closer and closer to You. Amen.

⬛ Embracing Your Calling—Day 2

1. What was God's original intent for relationship as shown in the Garden of Eden?

2. Why does God ask questions? Has God ever asked you a question? If so, what question did He ask?

3. What does being a "carrier of His presence" mean to you?

4. Tell Jesus of your desire to walk with Him in every moment of every day.

Coming into the Light

Can you imagine, after Adam and Eve had known God, and He knew them, how quickly the spiritual climate changed? As a result of their disobedience, they experienced instantaneous barriers to their intimacy with Him. Walls shot up. After their sin they plucked off leaves from the nearest bush as quickly as they could and sewed coverings for themselves. They were hiding from the Lord their Creator for the first time in their lives.

But God, in His passionate pursuit, was still drawing close. A new reaction stirred within them as He drew near. Previously they had run toward the sound of His footsteps. Now they ran in the other direction. Before, their response had been joy: "Oh, *wow*, it's Father!" Now it was dread and fear: "Oh, *no*, it's Father!" They were guilt-ridden. Never had they had such an emotional reaction or even such a thought before! They had not known condemnation or fear or shame. Now, as a result of their disobedience, they ran and hid from the voice of God (the prophetic, we could say).

Obviously these were real live leaves they picked and sewed together for their coverings. But we pick and choose covers and hiding places as well. And the moment we hide behind our defensive fig leaf mind-sets from the revelatory voice of God, the heart of God, the acts of God and the power of God, it starts getting extremely complicated.

Why? Because now we automatically filter the voice, presence and power of God through screens. If God's Word does finally penetrate our hearts or minds, it seems as though it has become diluted due to our abundant rationalization, analytical skepticism, theological theories of cessationism or traditional emotional barriers. We might not sew actual fig leaves, but the obstructions to fellowship over our hearts and souls shield us just as effectively (or ineffectively) from God's approaching presence.

Leaves We Hide Behind

May I point out some of the leaves we hide behind? They are progressive; hiding behind one set leads to our concealment behind the next as well.

The Ditch of Guilty Feelings

The first set of leaves that many hide behind is guilt. Some seem to stay there all their lives, like a car that has been sideswiped and is still sitting in the ditch years later. Sinful acts or mistakes from the past or present loom in their faces, but instead of running to their loving Savior and admitting their fault, they sprint in the opposite direction and hide out in the darkness of guilt. This hiding place is the breeding ground for condemnation, accusation and other ugly attitudes. But all these can be avoided through old-fashioned confession of sin and cleansing by the blood of our Lord Jesus Christ.

There are various categories of guilt: *real guilt* due to real sin; *exaggerated guilt* due to the combination of real sin and the work of "the accuser of our brethren" (Revelation 12:10); and *false guilt* as a result of the voice of the destroyer, releasing condemning, lying spirits (1 Kings 22:21–23; John 8:44; 10:10). All these forms of guilt are very real in the realm of our emotions.

The cure is simple and direct. First John 1:7 gives us the remedy: "If we walk in the Light as He Himself is in the Light, we have fellowship with one another, and the blood of Jesus His Son cleanses us from all sin." Step into the light. That is where we find cleansing. So I have a "word from the Lord" for you: Climb out of the ditch and run to the light of God's Word. "The truth will make you free" (John 8:32). Forgiveness, cleansing and healing love are waiting for you there.

The Masquerade of Hurts from the Past

The second layer of leaves that hide us from the love of God and keep us from intimacy with Him is the religious masquerade, concealing deep-seated hurts from the past. Religious people wear masks quite well, pretending all is well with their souls while holding the Lord, the very Lover of their lives, at arm's length. Pretenders we become, masquerading in the parade of hypocritical churchianity.

But the real Jesus came to heal the brokenhearted and set at liberty those who are bruised (see Isaiah 61:1; Luke 4:18–19). Jesus is our healer. We must take off our masks and let Him dig deep at times, touching the very source of our pain. Let Him probe and even pierce through the festering wounds to allow the light of His unchanging love to penetrate your being. Expose it to the light. Surrender. Forgive. Sow blessings to others instead. This is the way out of the masquerade—remaining open-faced before God, releasing mercy and forgiveness for hurts from the past and letting Him do the same.

The Onlooker's Bench of Fear

Let's consider a third tier of camouflage. We want to be part of things, enjoy life, step out and be used by the Lord. But our

39

woundedness, made more raw by the taunts of the enemy, keeps us on the bench looking on while others are enjoying being in the middle of the game. We become cautious observers afraid to run onto the playing field.

This is the area I have struggled with the most. What will I look like if I do this? What will others think of me? How well will I perform? But if we allow ourselves to be held back by the fear of rejection or the fear of authority or the opinions of others, eventually we will become people-pleasers, strangled by the anticipation of their opinions.

Hear me in this: If God can help *me* off the spectator's bench, He can help you, too. In the past my mind has been numbed by the belittling notions of what I expected others were thinking of me. Fear can paralyze us while authentic faith propels us forward. So trade in those fears; exchange them at the cross (see Isaiah 8:12–13). Be bold like a lion for Jesus' sake. *Do something!* Jump off the bench, tread on those spirits of intimidation (see Luke 10:19) and be more than a conqueror (see Romans 8:37).

Truly, the remedy is our Father's great love. Bask in the light of His unfathomable devotion—what the King James Version calls *lovingkindness*. Do a word study on it. Ask for a revelation of it.

Soak in the reality that "if God is for us, who is against us?" (Romans 8:31). He does not just tolerate you. You were not an accident waiting to happen. You were created in His image and for His pleasure (see Revelation 4:11). You are the object of His consuming love.

Negative Criticism

There is a fourth layer of fig leaves that we can use to protect our image. Before you know it, you are not only a spectator sitting on the bench; you are the umpire of the games. First you develop an old, wrinkled-up prune face; then you begin operating out of a religious spirit called criticism. You have your ten points by which you judge everything around you. Like the judges at the Olympics, you give scores to the participants of the games. You leave a particular gathering or event and say, "Well, it could have been better, if only. . . ." But you offered nothing to help it to be better. Why should you? You have already been there, done that and gotten the T-shirt.

Sorry, but these are the has-beens of yesterday's moves of God. They stopped moving forward and now they hold the job of negative, critical overseers of the playing field of today.

Ouch! Those are some tough words. But it takes the penetrating light of truth to blast away our protective shields. Truth may hurt for the moment, but when it is prayed and spoken with the motivation of love, it cleanses and sets us free. I might be speaking a bit pointedly, but I want us to be delivered from all entanglements so that God can usher in the coming prophetic revolution. I know you do, too.

The Stronghold of Imposed Limitations

This brings us to the fifth layer of leaves we hide behind—that of imposed limitations. In this stage we start believing the ridiculous lies of the devil about ourselves, and those lies become negative strongholds of the mind (see 2 Corinthians 10:4–6). Words not in alignment with the will and Word of God are transmitted from the enemy's camp to attack our minds. At times those thoughts are even planted by people in authority. Their effect is to confine us in spaces with low ceilings and false expectations. As we believe those evil reports or actual word curses spoken against us as "the way it will always be," we are shut into cramped, dark boxes. Proverbs 23:7 reminds us of the promise and the problem: "As [a person] thinketh in his heart, so is he" (KJV).

Ed Silvoso, in his marvelous book *That None Should Perish*, has given us a good working definition of such spiritual strongholds. They represent "a mind-set impregnated with hopelessness that causes us to accept as unchangeable situations that we know are contrary to the will of God."[1]

As we acknowledge as hopeless what God declares is changeable, we have come into alignment, at least in part, with the devil's thought processes and plans for us. In this fifth stage, we go way past the realms of guilt, woundedness, fear and criticism. We no longer want to step out into the light. We flat-out do not even think He accepts us, loves us or has any plan for us—even a plan B.

But this is simply not true. God loves you and He loves a fighter. You need to know that there are times you will have to wage war with the name and blood of Jesus to break out of your box of imposed limitations. But there *is* a way out. The gateway is the cross of our lovely Lord Jesus!

Opportunities and Temptations

As we back up in the book of Genesis, we hear the serpent telling Adam and Eve, "God knows that in the day you eat from [the fruit] your eyes will be opened, and you will be like God" (Genesis 3:5). So what did Eve do? "When the woman saw that the tree was good for food, and that it was a delight to the eyes, and that the tree was desirable to make one wise" (verse 6), she partook.

There are three statements here that represent both opportunities and temptations: The forbidden tree was good for food; it was a delight to the eyes; and it was desirable to make one wise.

We find similar enticements in 1 John 2:16–17: "All that is in the world, the lust of the flesh and the lust of the eyes and the boastful pride of life, is not from the Father, but is from the world. The world is passing away, and also its lusts; but the one who does the will of God lives forever." The original temptation is still centered in these very things: the lust of the eyes, the lust of the flesh and the boastful pride of life. As we yield to these false motives, we start erecting barriers around our eyes and our hands—the very tools God wants to use as receptacles for His great presence.

The Lust of the Eyes

God wants our vision to be clear and single. He wants His eyes to burn brightly through our own (see Ephesians 1:17–19; Revelation 1:14). But when we give our eyes away to the enemy's camp, they become filled with vain images and other distractions. What we are doing is allowing tainted filters and visual obstacles to block the prophetic presence. We are hiding, and the revelatory seer dimension in which the Lord wants us to walk—for example, through dreams, visions and angelic visitations—becomes hindered. As we give ourselves to the lust of the eyes, the seer realm starts getting cloudy. It gets smeared, jumbled and filled with distorted images, because the lenses through which we are looking are not pure.

"Blessed are the pure in heart, for they shall see God," Jesus taught in the Sermon of the Mount (Matthew 5:8). This is why it is imperative that we guard the "eye gate" and keep the eyes of our hearts clean and pure. This is why the god of this world (see John 14:30; 2 Corinthians 4:4) is sending a barrage of filth for the eyes of the world to behold. A battle is raging, the battle of passions. Will we let our eyes get filled with junk and poke out the prophetic gift of the seer in our midst? It will and does do that. But if we keep pure eyes, a realm of visionary revelation will open up with greater clarity for us.

I am not trying to present a work ethic or advocate earning God's grace and gifts. We cannot earn a present. But we must keep ourselves clean from the lust of the eyes in order to receive gracefully what the Father has to offer.

The Lust of the Flesh

The second temptation mentioned is the lust of the flesh. Oh, the impulses and temptations that this body creeps up and speaks to each of us! We must go through the cleansing and crucifying of the lust of the flesh. Do you know why? Because God wants His power to move through human vessels. He wants our hands to be clean and our hearts to be pure, as Psalm 24:3–4 describes: "Who may ascend into the hill of the LORD? And who may stand in His holy place? He who has clean hands and a pure heart."

When the eyes of our hearts are pure, we can behold Him; and as we do, His presence can move and work through our clean hands. We need to be a people cleansed of the lust of the eyes and purged from the lust of the flesh. What these temptations accomplish is getting us into a whole lot of wrong places, seeing wrong things and motivating us to do bad stuff.

Romans 6:13 exhorts us not to "go on presenting the members of your body to sin as instruments of unrighteousness; but present yourselves to God as those alive from the dead, and your members as instruments of righteousness to God." The issue becomes one of presentation. Your members become a slave to the one to whom you present them. If unto the Lord, then they become a slave to the Holy Spirit; if unto sin, they become slaves to sin. What a promise! What a warning!

Yes, what a promise. God wants to use our little hands to impart the power of His great presence. Is that not crazy?—your hands and mine used to release the power of His presence.

Romans 6:19 urges us to "present your members as slaves to righteousness, resulting in sanctification." Awesome! But that is God's way. As we present the members of our fleshly bodies to the Lord, He performs a miracle: He sanctifies them. That means these feet, hands, eyes, mouths and hearts become set apart for the Lord's glory and purposes. As we present, He sanctifies. What He sanctifies, He empowers. Then, like Isaiah, as we are touched by authentic fire, He will touch others through our lives with His miraculous fire. It does not get much better than that.

The Boastful Pride of Life

Then there is the boastful pride of life. Who gets the credit? Who receives the glory? In many ways boastful pride deals with false worship. Eve saw that the fruit was desirable to make one wise. But wise in whose eyes? Wise in comparison to ourselves, yes, and wise in comparison to others, but not wise in comparison to God.

The boastful pride of life, then, is actually a realm characterized by false worship. If you are walking in the boastful pride of life, ultimately it is an issue of self-exaltation. The basic meaning of *worship* in the Hebrew language means "to bow down in prostration before." Pride is the antithesis of worship. Worship exalts another, while pride sits on its own self-appointed throne.

I think I can hear the wheels of your mind grinding: "Okay, but what in the world does this have to do with the prophetic ministry?" My response: Everything! God has an address; it is called *p-r-a-i-s-e*. He is enthroned on the praises of His people (see Psalm 22:3).

The act of worship is one of our most powerful tools of spiritual warfare. It builds a throne in the heavenlies where Jesus' rule can be released and the demonic powers of darkness dismissed. Worship displaces darkness. So when you are walking in extravagant, passionate worship, guess what happens? Your passionate praise of our Lord pushes the throne of pride out of the way, and He comes to take His seat of honor. He draws near. Worship is prophetic action that releases the spirit opposite to the boastful pride of life.

I tell you the truth, as we enter into true worship, His presence comes. And in His presence we find *everything* (see Psalm

45

16:11). In His presence we can hear Him, feel Him, touch Him, know Him, see Him . . . and we might even smell Him—the beauty of His fragrance.

Praise has a whole lot to do, therefore, with a prophetic lifestyle of intimacy and ministry. It is connected with our giving God His rightful place in our lives, in our congregations and even in whole cities. In fact, extravagant praise is a key that unlocks His presence with us.

Take and Eat

As we close today's reading, let's return to Genesis, where the first "take-and eat" is given in the Bible. "Take and eat" was first spoken by the enemy to Adam and Eve (see Genesis 3:1–5). They disobeyed God and did as the sly serpent connived them into doing. Sin came, and with it, barriers to intimacy. But the next "take-and-eat" in the Bible is the remedy for us all: Jesus talking with His disciples.

Jesus said, giving them the bread, "Take it; this is my body" (Mark 14:22). The one great cure for all the barriers we hide behind is the take-and-eat of the cross of Jesus. It is "Take and eat" of the life of God's only Son. "Take and eat" of this glorious Man, Christ Jesus. He has already done it all. He gave His blood to purchase us all. As we revel in who Jesus is, God the Father wraps His arms around us, and we have this warm presence called passion within our hearts, and this thing called revelation that starts bubbling up and happening.

Jesus' friends will draw close to His chest to hear His very heartbeat. The lifestyle of a prophet is marked by intimacy, and an intimate life with Christ is available to you.

Jesus is looking for new recruits who will hear the passionate sound of His love beating through their beings. Want to lean your ear His way?

⟩ P R A Y E R ⟨

Dear Father, I desire to lean in with eager anticipation when I sense You are drawing near to me by Your Holy Spirit. I have covered myself in the past with my own version of fig leaves. I am now coming into Your light—the gracious light of Your countenance that shines upon me. I confess that I have been enticed by the lust of the eyes, the lust of the flesh and the pride of life. Forgive me. In response I praise You and thank You for the body and blood of Jesus that have been given for me so that I can walk in newness of life for the glory of Your Son, Jesus. Amen.

⟩ Embracing Your Calling—Day 3

1. What are barriers to intimacy in your life? What are the leaves you hide behind?

2. How have the three fleshly, world motivating forces from 1 John 2:16 affected your life?

3. In what way have you seen praise and worship as a prophetic action that releases the spirit opposite to pride?

4. Take a moment right now and present yourself to God and your members as "instruments of righteousness." Then release His presence within you through praise.

Character to Carry the Gift

Most prophets I know are real characters, for sure! From my vantage point, you must have a bit of an adventure streak in you just to survive the rapids in this whitewater rafting ride. It also requires the character of endurance to leave a lasting impression in the Christian life. A river without banks is just runoff water. The *charismata* (Holy Spirit gifts) without character are a swamped raft just waiting to happen. But when character is shaped in the image of Christ Jesus, then the presence, power and authority of the Holy Spirit have an effective course through which to be channeled.

Leonard Ravenhill, the esteemed late British evangelist, stated, "The prophet comes to set up that which is upset. His work is to call into line those who are out of line! He is unpopular because he opposes the popular in morality and spirituality. In a day of faceless politicians and voiceless preachers, there is not a more urgent national need than our cry to God for a prophet!"[1] Indeed, upholding morality is the job of a prophet. But doing this kind of work takes a tried and tested character to endure the storms that come.

Characteristics of Prophetic People

When we consider the stereotypical images of prophetic vessels, we might think of wrinkled old men with long, pointy fingers shouting vehemently outside the ranks of those whom they are addressing. Wearing ragged clothes, eating grasshoppers for meals, they pronounce their declarations of doom, then proceed to the next village to do the same. Their job: to judge the Church and help God out in the process, just in case He does not do a good enough job. This is definitely a distorted view of the lifestyle of a prophet!

Here are four more accurate pictures of prophetic people who are pursuing an intimate and godly walk with Christ.

They Are People of Genuine Faith

Abraham was captivated by God with a vision and purpose. But Hebrews 11:8–10 indicates that he stepped out "not knowing where he was going." With that thought in mind, might you fit the image of a prophetic person of faith?

God gives us hints. He gives us directions. But believe me, we still have to walk by faith, one step at a time. God often plays leapfrog in His spiritual alphabet with us, giving us just enough to get us going. He likes jumping onto the first lily pad in the pond of His purpose, the one marked *a*, *b* and *c*, and then jumping over to the pad with *l*, *m* and *n* posted on it. Next thing you know, the Holy Spirit's guidance reveals another hint to us of our divine destiny. Suddenly the goal of it all comes into view. Yes, we now see *x*, *y* and *z*. "Oh, boy!" we exult, getting all cranked up. "Look at that. I see it now." Then we hit *e*, *f* and *g*. "Huh? Whoa, baby, where is that next pad?"

This is reality. To me it sounds like the path Abraham took— the prophet, the friend of God, the father of our faith. While he was in the process of becoming that man of faith, taking progressive steps into the journey we call destiny, he kept looking because he had seen x, y and z. He had glimpsed something that was worth the cost of looking foolish and making mistakes along the way. He was willing to be a pioneer of faith to blaze a trail that others could follow.

Abraham was looking for something—actually, for Someone. Like all authentic prophetic pilgrims who came after him, he maintained his gaze upward. He kept looking for the city whose builder and architect was God.

With this set of lenses, you might see your circumstances differently and take courage. You might just qualify to be an authentic prophetic person—a man or woman of genuine faith.

They Are Pioneers Taking New Territory

Prophetic people are those who go before and open the way for others. They are called pioneers, forerunners or "breakers" in the spirit. They pay the price, often as intercessors, plowing up fallow ground so that others can follow in their trail as sowers, planters, waterers and eventually reapers. Micah 2:13 describes this activity: "The breaker goes up before them; they break out, pass through the gate and go out by it. So their king goes on before them, and the LORD at their head." Before there is a breakthrough, there must always come a breaker.

The world has its hit squads that do the dirty work. Send those guys in and get your job done. So it is with the prophetic. These commandos, armed with the tools of spiritual warfare, kick down the gates of the enemy so that spoils can be taken for the Kingdom of God. The grace of a John the Baptist or an Elijah seems to be upon these warriors, and they, too, become forerunners, preparing the way for the release of the Lord's presence.

Pioneers they truly are. They love the task of plowing new territory, but they cannot wait till the next round of gifted laborers appears, relieving them of their temporary responsibilities. Bad settlers they were born to be; spiritual boredom sets in if they tend one field for too long. So they revel when another takes over the tasks they themselves began. Fresh grace seems to appear as a glint in their eyes over a new assignment revealed. These prophetic pioneers are paying the price as groundbreakers.

Know this for sure—if you are going to be a prophetic person, sooner or later you will be used with a plow in your hand.

They Are Messengers with a Clear Word

Prophetic people carry a living word of not being conformed to this world, and they wield this message masterfully like a sharp, two-edged sword. T. Austin Sparks states it this way: "Prophetic ministry under the Holy Spirit is a ministry through growing revelation. A prophet was a man who went back to God again and again and did not come out to speak until God had shown him the next thing."[2] Messengers carry a word with them. Their job is to be mouthpieces on behalf of another. Anna's prophetic message, as recorded in Luke 2:38, was simple; she "continued to speak of [Jesus]." He is our message!

Here is a good image, then, to reflect on: True messengers speak and live the message of the cross. Ultimately the cross must be our passion (see 1 Corinthians 1:23; 2:2). We must preach Jesus Christ crucified and risen from the dead. That goes against the grain in a godless society. But there is no deeper life message than the simplicity and centrality of the cross.

The power of God rests not on the wisdom, articulation and education of men and women, but on the foolishness of the preaching of the cross. The Lord wants to bring us back into proper focus. We are to be people with a message. Is it possible that you could qualify for such a simple yet profound task?

They Are Members of a Servant Community

In contrast to much Old Testament stereotyping, these radical warriors do not walk alone. They are not isolated individuals, though they often thrive on seclusion. They are a people knit together relationally as part of the greater Body of Christ. They are connected to the community of believers called the Church. They are members of a servant community.

The Church at large is to be a prophetic people. Remember the hot, piercing words of Moses: "Would that all the LORD's people were prophets, that the LORD would put His Spirit upon them!" (Numbers 11:29). How else will the slumbering giant awaken unless some revelatory dynamite is set off right in the middle of her?

We are all called by God. But we are not called to be lone rangers. Nor are there supposed to be a few elite, awesome superstars in the Church. We are *all* called to walk in the anointing of a word of knowledge or wisdom, His character and His power. We are called to do it together. First Peter 4:10 reminds us, "As each one has received a special gift, employ it in serving one another as good stewards of the manifold grace of God." This has the sound of a prophetic servant community to me.

When you study the armor of God in Ephesians, you will see that one area of your body is not protected. That is your hind side. Somebody else covers it for you, according to the book of Joel:

> They run like mighty men, they climb the wall like soldiers; and they each march in line, nor do they deviate from their paths. They do not crowd each other, they march everyone in his path; when they burst through the defenses, they do not break ranks.
>
> Joel 2:7–8

If you are marching in an army, somebody is striding in front of you and someone behind you, watching your heels. In a sense, then, part of your armor is not just the shield of faith or the breastplate of righteousness, but the people you are in step with. That means *you* are part of the armor for someone else, too! You might be prophetic eyes for another soldier, to guard him, watch for him, pray for him, love and care for him, remind him, heal him, comfort him, even kick and prod him so he will not collapse. Others, in turn, are your rearguard and will spur you on as well. That is what it means to be part of a servant community of believers.

Cultivating Character: Fruit That Is Grown

Have you ever noticed how many excruciating lessons there are to learn in character development? It is so good to remember that *God does not want us only to give a message; He wants us to become a living word.* Because the revelatory-gifted person is extra-sensitive, he or she must give the area of character development special attention. The cross of Christ will eventually become the love of any true prophetic person.

In his excellent book *Prophets, Pitfalls and Principles*, Dr. Bill Hamon shares an illustration from agriculture to drive home a spiritual point concerning character issues. A weed called Johnson grass intertwines its roots with the root system of a good crop, such as corn (to which it looks almost identical). The weed steals nutrients from the corn, but it cannot be pulled up by the roots without destroying the corn. The result: a scrawny, inferior crop, unsuited to be used as a seed corn for the next planting. Only after the harvest can the problem be fixed, when the farmer can plow up the earth to expose and remove the roots of the weed.

> In the spiritual realm as well, God will not deal with advanced root problems during a productive ministry season. He will bring the ministry . . . into a winter season of inactivity and

non-productivity. He will plow the prophet upside down, exposing the root problems, and then He will either spray them with a strong anointing to destroy them or else rake the minister's soul until all the roots are removed and thrown into the fire of God's purging purpose.

For that reason we must allow God and those He has appointed as our spiritual overseers to show us our weed/seed attitudes and remove the newly sprouted character flaws before they grow intertwined with our personality and performance. The longer we wait, the more drastic the process becomes.[3]

Growing in the prophetic—hearing God's voice, receiving visions, knowing His heart and so on—is extremely simple. At times we overly complicate this scene. It is a relational issue. Just hang out with Jesus; He likes talking to His friends. Growing in character requires the same strategy. The focus of the prophetic is being with God and learning to lean our heads on our Beloved, as the disciple John did. It is showing up and being where God is. It is not hiding but relating. Bottom line, that is how all this wonderful activity takes place. Remember, it is not what you know but *whom* you know.

Here are some keys I have been learning over the past 35-plus years of ministry in cultivating God's prophetic presence in my life. There are not seven effective steps to being a successful prophet—not that I know of, anyway. But here are seven helpful hints that have been milestones along my own journey of cultivating intimacy and growing in character in the prophetic.

1. *Rest around the Ark.* Where did the voice of the Lord come to young Samuel (see 1 Samuel 3:3–4), who became the last of the judges and one of the greatest prophets ever? In the Temple near the Ark of God. Be like little boy Samuel and find your resting place near the Ark of His presence. Learn to rest in the presence of God.

2. *Love mercy.* Mercy is a quality of the heart. If we do not have it, we will judge by the externals and be moved by opinions rather than by the Spirit of God (see 1 Samuel 16:7; Titus 3:4–7). Let Micah 6:8 be your goal: "He has told you, O man, what is good; and what does the LORD require of you but to do justice, to love kindness, and to walk humbly with your God?"

3. *Pray in the Spirit.* Fresh revelation will be released to you as you edify yourself and recharge your battery of faith by praying in the Holy Spirit (see 1 Corinthians 14:4). "[Build yourself] up on your most holy faith, praying in the Holy Spirit, keep [yourself] in the love of God" (Jude 20–21).

4. *Inquire of the Lord.* The key to learning is asking. The key to receiving is listening. The key to revelation is inquiring of the Lord (see Psalm 27:4, 8–14). Keep looking, asking, searching and inquiring of the Lord for Him to reveal truth, revelation and insight. He will answer a seeking, teachable heart.

5. *Learn to hold a secret.* Everything you receive as revelation does not come with an automatic license to share it. God reveals His secrets "to His servants the prophets" (Amos 3:7), but learn to ask permission whether you are to communicate them or not. God is looking for close friends He can share His secrets with.

6. *Love the anointing.* If you want to grow in the gifting and "gracelets" of God, then love the manifested presence of the Lord (see Exodus 33:15–16; 1 John 2:27). Cultivate His presence and anointing in your life by getting into the atmosphere where the Holy Spirit is moving. Some things are better caught than taught.

7. *Risk!* Fruit is borne out on the limb. Eventually we have to move out of our comfort zones and step out in faith. Remember, faith is always spelled *r-i-s-k*. Keep taking these

progressive steps and you will grow (see Romans 10:17; Hebrews 4:2; 11:6). Climb out of your boat and trust the Lord. He loves to go on adventures with His friends.

Character Signs along the Way

The writer of Hebrews finished his letter with these words: "Now the God of peace . . . equip you in every good thing to do His will, working in us that which is pleasing in His sight, through Jesus Christ" (Hebrews 13:20–21). It is through Jesus Christ that He equips us, develops our character and works in us what is well pleasing. Here are ten points to consider as God takes you through this often-challenging process:

1. Seldom is character seen until pressures and trials come. At such times gifts may dry up and even disappear for a season, as the pruning of the Lord takes place in the character of the gifted vessel.

2. As character matures, it greatly enhances the individual and his or her gift and calling.

3. Because of its invisible nature, character can be harder to gauge, in terms of progress and growth, than a grace gift from God.

4. Self-awareness of personal motives is very hard to recognize. It is possible for a person to give a true word with an impure motive of self-promotion that is not detected by the one giving the word. Let's be kind and not judgmental with each other. God is faithful to deal with each person's character in His way and in His time.

5. In time you come to understand not to sacrifice long-term goals to achieve short-term success.

6. Learn to value "team life." Realize you need others to help watch out for you, your family and your priorities.

Become accountable in motives, finances, morality and other major areas of natural and spiritual life.

7. In character development you learn to honor others and not envy their positions, titles, functions, prestige or gifting. You learn that before honor comes humility.

8. You learn to overcome jealousy and wait on His timing in your life. The Lord spoke to Jeremiah, for example, in about 627 BC (the thirteenth year of Josiah), yet it was not until 612 BC that he began to prophesy. He waited fifteen years. The next year, in 611 BC, sixteen years after Jeremiah's visitation by the Lord, certain tablets of the Law were found. Yet King Josiah did not consult Jeremiah about their meaning, but the prophetess Huldah (see 2 Kings 22:8–14; 2 Chronicles 34:14–15, 19–22).

9. Learn to give mercy and grace to others as they, too, are Christians under construction. This, in turn, sows a crop of mercy and understanding from others to you.

10. Give all glory, honor and praise to the Lord. Your weaknesses will glare in front of you, driving you into greater intimacy with the Lord. Embrace the cross, refuse the temporal adulation of others and revel in His unconditional love.

Go for the Double!

For years I have encouraged prophetic people to go for "the double." Many have cried out to the Lord for a double portion in the likeness of Elisha receiving a double portion from Elijah. The double I am talking about is the full expression of Christ's *character* combined with the full expression of His resurrection *power*. Now that is the double portion I want, and that is the double portion I entreat you to pursue.

⊨ P R A Y E R ⊨

Lord Jesus, I desire to be a person of genuine faith—a pioneer taking new territory, declaring the word of the Lord with clarity, love and a servant's heart. My heart wanders and I want to go my own way. Help me to stay close to You and grow in strength of character. I want to share Your Word, and I also want to be Your living word. I am going for the double—fullness of the likeness of Christ expressed in my life in both godly character and resurrection power. I want to be like You, Jesus. You are beautiful. Amen.

⊨ Embracing Your Calling—Day 4

1. What wrong images of the prophetic have caused you to shy away from fully embracing the prophetic gift on your life?

2. Which two of the seven hints for cultivating character and intimacy are most applicable to you right now? Why?

3. Which character signs have you seen in your life? Which are you seeing right now?

4. Tell Jesus that you want to walk in "the double": the full expression of His character and His power. Ask Him which of the seven hints for cultivating character He wants you to focus on right now. Commit yourself to pursue this area and allow Him to work this into your character. Then ask Him to confirm this word with His power in your life.

Awakened and Authentic

In the movie *The Matrix*, the characters have to choose between a red or blue pill—and it is very important which pill they
choose. I once had a dream where two close-fisted hands turned
downward came before me. I knew that inside each fist was an
important message and I had to choose correctly. A voice said,
"Make your choice." I looked at both hands and heard myself
say, "I choose right. I choose the right hand."

The right hand then turned over in the dream and the fingers
opened up to reveal a white capsule. The pill was placed in my
right hand, and I began to bring it to my mouth. As I did, I saw
that there was a word written on the pill. The word was *Awake*.
I knew instinctively that it was important in the days ahead that
we be alert to make wise life choices in the fear of the Lord.

I had actually "awakened" early that particular morning and
then I sensed from the Holy Spirit that I was to linger in bed for
a moment. Suddenly, it seemed, I fell into a deep sleep and was
given this impacting revelatory encounter. Then I was awakened
right at the exact right time—just in time to get ready for my
appointment to teach that day. I woke up just in time!

It is time for an awakening to occur in the Body of Christ to let our light penetrate this present darkness. We must choose wisely so that we can fully walk in God's assignment for each of us.

Did you realize that it is possible to be living a lifestyle of intimacy and still be asleep when you should be awake? John, the disciple who I believe had the most intimate relationship with Christ, fell asleep—three times—when asked to "watch and pray" with Jesus during a night of great agony in the Garden of Gethsemane (see Matthew 26:36–46). We, too, even amidst our pursuit of a lifestyle of intimacy, need to be awakened to the hour in which we live. It is time to wake up from our sleep and walk as authentic followers of Jesus Christ.

Authentic Characteristics

In our search for authentic characteristics of those who carry a prophetic gift, let's take a look at Romans 13:11–14:

> Do this, knowing the time, that it is already the hour for you to awaken from sleep; for now salvation is nearer to us than when we believed. The night is almost gone, and the day is near. Therefore let us lay aside the deeds of darkness and put on the armor of light. Let us behave properly as in the day, not in carousing and drunkenness, not in sexual promiscuity and sensuality, not in strife and jealousy. But put on the Lord Jesus Christ, and make no provision for the flesh in regard to its lusts.

I want to give you seven signs of being an awakened prophetic person, based on this passage.

1. They Are Spiritually Alert

I know a prophetic minister who had an angel visit him during a personal retreat. According to his testimony, the angel stood at the foot of his bed, blew the shofar and said one word: "Awake!" The word to the Church is the same: *Awake!*

The prophetic ministry in particular is supposed to blow a trumpet in the ears of the Church and cause her to arise. The apostle Paul is saying this in the above passage: "It's time to wake up, Church!" The King James Version translates this phrase in verse 11, "It is high time." I like that. It is high time for us to wake up out of sleep. If we are spiritually awake, then all our senses are alert and working. We are not dozing off on the job, but attentive and ready to respond.

2. They Cast Off Darkness

"Let us therefore cast off the works of darkness" is the way the King James Version puts verse 12. The NASB says we are to "lay aside the deeds of darkness." The issue is this: An authentic prophetic person is among those who cast off the works of darkness. We are to lay them aside. As Ephesians 5:7–10 remarks, "Do not be partakers with them; for you were formerly darkness, but now you are Light in the Lord; walk as children of Light (for the fruit of the Light consists in all goodness and righteousness and truth), trying to learn what is pleasing to the Lord."

If you are prophetic, that means you are going against the grain. It means you live a holy life, swimming against the current of mainstream society. That distinction means more than just your living up to a code of dos and don'ts. You have a Helper who not only supports you as you cast away the excess baggage, but lives within you and will do it through you.

When God puts His presence on His people, it becomes the outstanding distinguishing characteristic that sets them apart from all others (see Exodus 33:16). He makes us different because He is different. We can then cast off the deeds of darkness because, simply put, the Helper is helping out.

The phrase *cast off* has a particular action connotation. It is not displaying passivity, but showing an aggressive act on our side as well. When you cast something off, you take it and throw it as fast and as hard away from you as you can. Cast off those deeds of darkness with a fast fling. We cannot afford to keep them around.

3. They Are an Army of Light

Because we are fighting in a real war, we are also to "put on the armor of light" (verse 12) and walk in the light. Put on this Man, Christ Jesus (see Galatians 3:27, KJV). He is the greatest warrior of all time and the Captain of heaven's army.

Jesus is really good at drafting people into that army. My dear, deceased wife, Michal Ann, was given a dream in which the Holy Spirit was looking for prophetic mentors—mothers and fathers in the Spirit. In this dream she was standing in line with a bunch of people, and the Holy Spirit was saying, "Whoever wants to volunteer to be a father or a mother in the prophetic, I want you to step forward." My wife continued to stand in the line, as everybody else took a step back. She continued standing there all alone, making it appear that she had stepped forward. The Holy Spirit said, "You volunteered!" She pondered, *I volunteered?* Then a wind came from behind and flung her forward. "Yes," God said, "you volunteered!"

Jesus wants us constantly to reenlist for the army of God (see Psalm 110:3) and put on the armor of light. Displace darkness by walking in the light. What is the light? It is truth. Truth is not just correct doctrine; it is truthfulness worked into our innermost parts. We are a volunteer army and our effective weaponry is truth—not just by what we speak, but by what we live out.

Christ Jesus is still alive today and wants to live His radical life through you. Hey, be distinctly different! Arise! Shake off passivity and be a consecrated warrior for our Lord. Does He deserve anything less?

4. They Live Transparent and Honest Lives

The KJV puts Romans 13:13 like this: "Let us walk honestly, as in the day." The NASB renders it, "Let us behave properly as in the day." Do you know what the world is looking for? Definitely not Christians who say they have their acts together but really do not. No, the world would rather see a people who are in process and admit it. That builds a bridge from the Church to the world—a bridge called honesty and transparency. It is a span we need to build because the world is looking for people who are real. We can then direct seekers, in hope, to the One who is changing us.

True prophetic people are not just a bunch of folks going along with the latest trend. Real Christians are not fakes. It is not always easy to be honest and transparent and open, but it is breathtakingly refreshing.

I am learning a principle dealing with the impartation of spiritual life. The more transparent and honest I am, the more life is imparted to others. Transparency and honesty are aspects of intimacy and they build hope in people. When I allow others to see my brokenness, struggles and process, they can relate to the pressures I am going through, yet see that I continue to walk on. That gives them hope that they, too, can continue on the journey of becoming. And something deeper than teaching occurs. Impartation happens, then relational transparency.

5. They Flee Carnality

"Not in rioting and drunkenness, not in chambering and wantonness, not in strife and envying" (Romans 13:13, KJV). "Not in carousing and drunkenness, not in sexual promiscuity and sensuality, not in strife and jealousy" (NASB). Is it not intriguing that, right in the same group of sexual issues to be dealt with, we find strife and jealousy?

It is no coincidence. They are partners with spiritual adultery. Yes, strife and jealousy cause divisions and breakups in ministries and churches. You become jealous of what someone else has in contrast to what you possess. You want that person's car, his house, his job, his physique, his spouse, his calling or ministry. Your envy arises out of insecurity over your own identity.

But let's not be sowers of strife and competition or motivated by selfish ambition. When I say to avoid carnal living, I am not referring just to the outward issues. I am including the attitudes of the heart: motivations, ambitions, lusts. We must cast off competition, ambition, jealousy and strife, as well as party spirit, sensuality and sexual promiscuity. Let's run as fast as we can in the opposite direction. Let's scurry to the Lord and cry, "Help!" May He purify our hearts so that our hands can be clean.

6. They Lean on Jesus

The next sign of an awakened prophetic people is probably the most strategic. The KJV aptly phrases it, "Put ye on the Lord Jesus Christ" (verse 14). He is our message. He is our life. Let's put on and demonstrate and exhibit this Man, our source and strength for living.

Notice once again the study in contrasts. When we admit our weaknesses, Jesus provides the remedy of His very own strength. He is our everything, and He loves for His people to be dependent on Him. Yes, we are weak but He is strong.

Remember John, the disciple of Jesus, who learned this in the process of becoming a true disciple. After a few years of life in the trenches of ministry, he leaned his head on the heart of Jesus. What do you think? Could you learn to do the same?

Leaning on Jesus is the most prophetic thing that anyone can do, and it does not require a special gift.

7. They Keep Their Priorities Right

"Make not provision for the flesh, to fulfil the lusts thereof" (verse 14, KJV). "Ouch!" you might respond, as the conviction of the Holy Spirit settles on your soul. Do you know what this has to do with? When nobody is watching. When you are on a trip. When you are in that hotel room. When you are away from your parents or at college. When you are home alone. I have a word for you: Keep your priorities right. After all, Someone is watching over your shoulder. Be the real thing. Have the real content in the can. Never be a fake.

Here, then, is the issue: Be wise. Do not give the flesh or the devil an inch. He always tries to get extra mileage out of any deal. Do not let him. Any void or vacuum always gets filled up with something. If you squelch the prophetic nature of the Holy Spirit, then the opposites of these seven characteristics will come into play. This opens the door for the Jezebel spirit to romp through our midst.

This demonic spirit hates the prophetic and seeks to destroy God-ordained authority. It causes fear, debilitating discouragement, depression and immobilization (see 1 Kings 16:31; 18:4, 19; 19:1–4; 21:5–19, 25–27; 2 Kings 9:7–10; 22–37; Revelation 2:20–23). Perversions of many kinds will be the outcome.

So keep your priorities right and make no allowance for the flesh or the devil. Always bask in the culture of grace!

The Power of Choice

So along with me, let's choose Him who sits at the right hand. Let's choose righteousness. Let's choose to dream for a while. Together, let's partake of the medicine contained within the pill called "awake" and arise into the fullness of being an authentic prophetic people. Dare we strive for anything less?

PRAYER

Father, I want to be an authentic prophetic person who talks the talk and walks the walk. Help me to be a pilgrim of faith—a pioneer breaking open new territory and a messenger with a clear word. Awaken any part of me that is dull or has fallen asleep. Fashion me into a real, transparent follower of Jesus Christ who flees carnality by running into the safety of Your arms of love. Grant me the grace to stay in the race for the long haul and not treat Your presence as if it were the latest fad. Help me keep my priorities right. I want to be all that You want me to be for Your great name's sake. Amen.

Embracing Your Calling—Day 5

1. What do you consider some of the authentic characteristics of prophetic people?

2. If you were to ask the Lord to strengthen you in one particular area, what would it be and why?

3. According to Romans 13:11–14, what are some of the characteristics of prophetic people?

4. Talk to Jesus and ask Him to strengthen your character in one or two of the seven areas from Romans 13:11–14. Remember, leaning on Jesus is the most prophetic thing that anyone can do, and it does not require a special gift. So lean on Him and His strong everlasting arms.

Lovers of the Cross

Although receiving and releasing spiritual gifts is an important part of the package, the mature prophetic person has as his or her goal a lot more than being God's mail carrier. Being a prophet has to do first with intimate friendship with God, with having a heart passionately on fire with the Lord Jesus Christ. And if we are going to be a friend of God, we must be lovers of the cross.

James 4:4 strongly admonishes us, "You adulteresses, do you not know that friendship with the world is hostility toward God? Therefore whoever wishes to be a friend of the world makes himself an enemy of God." There is no way you can be a friend of God if you are not also a friend of the cross.

What does it mean to be lovers of the cross? T. Austin Sparks said:

> We cannot have the knowledge of the Lord—the most important thing in the mind of God for us—except on the ground of the continuous application of the Cross, and that will go right on to the end. Do not imagine that there will come a day when you have done with the Cross, when the principle of the Cross will no longer be necessary and when you have graduated from

the school where the Cross is the instrument of the Lord. Such a day never will be! If you are going on into greater fullness of knowledge—I mean spiritual knowledge of the Lord—and therefore greater fullness of usefulness to Him, you must take it as settled that the principle of the Cross is going to be applied more and more deeply as you go on.[1]

Friendship with God

Abraham is the first person identified in Scripture as a prophet (see Genesis 20:7). We call him the father of faith, the first of the patriarchs, a man of the covenant and other noteworthy titles. But the Scriptures mention another important thing about this man: He was called "the friend of God" (James 2:21–23; see also 2 Chronicles 20:7; Isaiah 41:8).

Abraham's friendship with God is borne out in Scripture by his many close encounters of an intimate kind. Is that what you want to see happen in your life, too? More than anything in my life, I want to be a friend of God. But if we are not friends of the cross, we are at enmity with God.

Now the one entity I truly want on my side is God Himself! I do not want to fight Him. When I choose the cross of Jesus, I am choosing friendship with God. Galatians 6:14 reminds us, "May it never be that I would boast, except in the cross of our Lord Jesus Christ, through which the world has been crucified to me, and I to the world." Paul is not speaking of a whimsical attitude toward the application of the cross in our lives; he is referring to the cross as our lifestyle.

Called to act in a spirit opposite to the spirit of this world by embracing Christ's cross as our own is the heart of the prophetic, the gate into greater and more intimate friendship with our Creator and the lover of our souls.

What do good friends do? They like hanging out with one another. They have a relationship that has become established over a period of time. Two new friends are often melded together through surviving the tensions of good times and bad. All significant relationships are tested through the trial of fire. Trust is not a spiritual gift; it has to be built over time. Once trust has been nurtured, faithful friends enter another level in their relationship. They begin to share their heart-kept secrets one with another.

So it is with the prophetic: "Surely the Lord GOD does nothing unless He reveals His secret counsel to His servants the prophets" (Amos 3:7). One of the great blessings in this life is to hear the Lord's voice. Lean your ear His way and let Him share with you wonderful words of life. In his book *Prophetic Ministry* Rick Joyner elaborates on that verse in Amos: "The Lord does not want to do anything without sharing it with the prophets, because the prophets are His friends. . . . The essence of prophetic ministry is to be the special friend and confidant of God."[2]

May friendship with God be your aim, while you "earnestly desire spiritual gifts, but especially that you may prophesy" (1 Corinthians 14:1). Usually this kind of relationship—walking in the shadow of the cross as your prophetic lifestyle—takes some time to cultivate. Crucified servants make no special claim to be heard, but they speak, act and are content to leave the matter there, confident not in themselves, but that they have heard from God and that every word from the Lord will find fulfillment.

Now *that* deals with the mature package of the prophetic! The problem is, most of us do not initially respond that way; we take it personally if we feel our word has not been received. Then we end up defensive, antagonistic and a little unfriendly in the process.

Our responsibility, however, is not whether or not a particular word is received. It is standing in the counsel of God—listening to His voice alone—and then bringing forth His heart with character, honoring spiritual authority and relating in a teachable manner. We can be confident that if it is His word, He will bear witness to it. God's thoughts are not our thoughts; His ways are not our ways. But when His word goes forth, it will not return void, but will accomplish the purposes for which He sent it forth (see Isaiah 55:8–11).

A Mouthful of Splinters

Hebrews 12:1–2 (NKJV) says:

> Since we are surrounded by so great a cloud of witnesses, let us lay aside every weight, and the sin which so easily ensnares us, and let us run with endurance the race that is set before us, looking unto Jesus, the author and finisher of our faith. . .

Slow down; watch this next phrase now:

> . . . who for the joy set before Him endured the cross, despising the shame and has sat down at the right hand of the throne of God.

I am thankful that this verse says Jesus *endured* the cross; it does not say it was fun or easy. It also gives us a hint of *how* He endured it. Jesus could see what was coming as a result of embracing the cross: "For the joy set before Him." Paul told us that *death works in us that life might work in others* (2 Corinthians 4:12). So look beyond the cross and see what lies on the other side. As you do, joy and strength will come, and you will be supernaturally enabled to bear your cross with joy.

Because there is a cross tailor-made for every one of us. It is shaped with just you in mind. (He knows how to make it fit, too.) The rich young ruler of Matthew 19 had a cross made specifically for him. Jesus said to no other person what He said to that wealthy young man: "You've done well. Now sell all that you have and give it to the poor."

The problem is, we tend to get legalistic and try to make a specific word from Jesus fit everyone else. Then we end up offering an admonition like, "You've got to sell everything and give it all to the poor." Believe me, we need a whole lot bigger heart of compassion for the poor. But that was a specific word to a specific person. The prophetic presence was being released through Jesus at that moment, exposing the idol in the young man's heart. It must have been the issue he struggled with the most: bowing down at the altar of mammon. Jesus was offering him the cross tailored just for him. But he turned away because it was too hard. He could not see beyond the cross to what lay ahead on the other side.

Jesus has a revelatory word that will cut right through to where you need it most. That sharp, piercing message will be different for you than for anybody else. What He asks you to give up and what He asks you to carry will not be exactly the same as for the next person.

Years ago I was deeply touched by a message calling us to have "A Mouthful of Splinters." Sounds terrible, right? But the Lord wants us to kiss the cross, to embrace the cross, to love the cross. It is your friend, not your enemy. It is true: Body piercing saved our lives. So kiss the cross and get a mouthful of splinters.

Classic Statements on the Cross

Dr. Bill Hamon, founder of Christian International and author of several books, has many years under his belt understanding the centrality of the cross in the life of the prophetic person. Let's take a look at what this pioneer has to say:

> The principal players in the biblical story—God, humanity, and the devil—are still the principal players today, and

though we live under a new covenant, these characters have not changed. God still speaks through His prophets, people still resent and resist God's prophetic word, and the devil still does all he can to destroy the prophets. So persecution and suffering are all part of the prophet's cross to bear. Jesus said that unless we are willing to take up our crosses and deny ourselves, we cannot be disciples (Mt. 16:24). How much more does this principle apply to being prophets? Prophets must take up their ministry crosses joyfully, denying themselves all the fleshly indulgences of these prophetic pitfalls, weed seed attitudes and syndromes.[3]

Two other prophetic statesmen of our day are John and Paula Sandford, founders of Elijah House Ministries. Their book *The Elijah Task: A Call to Today's Prophets* is one of the classic texts that many in my generation cut our teeth on. Here is what this wise couple had to say about embracing the cross:

> End-time prophets must be thoroughly dead to themselves in our Lord and risen to perfect obedience. Their minds must be purely in Him, lest they cast water on fires God is building, or worse yet, call for fires of suffering out of their own hidden desires for vengeance. The necessity of discipline is thus heavy upon us. Any fire, spiritual or earthly, is most difficult to control. Yes, controlled fires have warmed our houses, cooked our food and driven our engines. Controlled spiritual fire is even more necessary and valuable. Men must learn, as Paul did, to let affliction work its weight of gold.[4]

Let's also look at what Ed Dufresne, in a lighter and yet convicting fashion, relates in his book *The Prophet: Friend of God*:

> I once asked myself, "What am I doing, living in a hotel room? I could be home with my wife and my son!" And the Spirit of the Lord rose up in my spirit and said, "Dead men don't gripe." You know what happens to a living sacrifice? It dies. Dead

men never fight back, either. . . . Dead men never get even. . . .
Prophets must give up their bodies as a living sacrifice. Even
today they throw stones at prophets. Some of you say, "Yes, I
want the prophet's ministry." Will you still want it when things
like this happen? Will you still be willing to "present your bodies a living sacrifice, holy, acceptable unto God, which is your
reasonable service"?[5]

Last, let's hear from Dr. Michael L. Brown, author, instructor and revivalist. This contemporary statesman is calling for
a holy war on complacency in the Church:

> Our Savior made this perfectly clear, establishing two founda-
> tions for battle. The first foundation is, *Take up your cross.*
> The second foundation is, *Put down your sword.* We tend to
> get things reversed! We take up our sword, relying on human
> methods to change the world, and we put down our cross, de-
> spising God's method to change the world. God's method runs
> counter to the flesh. God's method seems weak and foolish.
> God's method flies in the face of established wisdom. God's
> method seems doomed to failure and defeat, yet it is the only
> way to succeed and win. God's method is the Cross![6]

Classic Scriptures on the Cross

Having looked at these in-your-face statements from some of
our veterans, let's load our guns with the original ammunition,
by way of Scripture statements from Jesus Himself and His
apostolic follower Paul. Do not try to avoid getting nailed right
now. As you read these verses, just lift up your hands, give up
and surrender to the Commander-in-Chief:

> "Anyone who does not take his cross and follow me is not wor-
> thy of me."
>
> Matthew 10:38, NIV

"If anyone wishes to come after Me, he must deny himself, and take up his cross and follow Me. For whoever wishes to save his life will lose it, but whoever loses his life for My sake and the gospel's will save it."

Mark 8:34–35

We who are alive are always being given over to death for Jesus' sake, so that His life may be revealed in our mortal body. So then, death is at work in us, but life is at work in you.

2 Corinthians 4:11–12, NIV

May it never be that I would boast, except in the cross of our Lord Jesus Christ, through which the world has been crucified to me, and I to the world.

Galatians 6:14

Brethren, join in following my example, and observe those who walk according to the pattern you have in us. For many walk, of whom I often told you, and now tell you even weeping, that they are enemies of the cross of Christ, whose end is destruction, whose god is their appetite, and whose glory is in their shame, who set their minds on earthly things.

Philippians 3:17–19

Ouch! and *Amen!* Nothing cuts and heals like the Word of God.

Embrace the Cross

Gifts can be imparted, but you must embrace the cross for yourself. No one else can do it for you. Embracing the cross involves dying to what is good in order that something better can come forth. This is the pattern of the prophetic lifestyle and the test for all who long for the progressive purposes of God. Death works in us that life might work in others.

The Lord is not looking for two or three awesomely gifted people with detailed words of knowledge to wow the crowds. The Holy Spirit is searching for people who will spend intimate time with their Father and waste their lives on Him. I would love to increase in many prophetic arenas, but that is not my major goal anymore. My aim is to be a friend of God, to lean my head on Jesus' chest, to love the cross, to have a mouthful of splinters.

I also long to see an intimate, passionate, consecrated generation of warriors of the cross—servant believers who are enflamed with love for their Messiah, whose walk is a crosscurrent within society, who release His fragrance of life and presence in whatever they do and wherever they go.

Some years ago, having gone through a difficult time of trials and emotional bruising, I had a dream in which different figures from Church history came and stood before me—people like John Huss, Martin Luther and Count Nikolaus Ludwig von Zinzendorf, benefactor of the Moravians. Then the scene changed to modern times and a well-known prophet of our day faced me. His words pierced my being: "The glory of the cross is to bear your pain without defending yourself." I woke up stunned, not condemned but inspired, knowing what the Lord required of me in that season. I was grateful. I was shocked. I was relieved. And I was shown the way out of my dilemma—the way of the cross.

Let me conclude this reading with the majestic words of the first verse of another great hymn, this one written by Thomas Shepherd in 1693: *Must Jesus Bear the Cross Alone?* It needs no explanation!

> Must Jesus bear the cross alone,
> And all the world go free?
> No, there's a cross for ev-'ry one,
> And there's a cross for me.

⟩ PRAYER ⟨

Precious Holy Spirit, clarify my vision of the cross of Christ. I want to be Your friend, and I want to be a friend of the cross. I choose to follow You—to deny myself, take up my cross each day and walk the narrow path with You by my side. I ask that the cross would be central to my prophetic lifestyle of intimacy. Lord Jesus, I lay aside every weight and sin that easily entangles me, and I fix my eyes upon You so that I can run with endurance the race You have put before me. Help me to live a life worthy of the calling You have given to me for Your great honor and fame. Amen.

⧫ Embracing Your Calling—Day 6

1. What does friendship with God look like to you?

2. What does it mean to you, practically speaking, to deny self, pick up your cross and follow Jesus?

3. Jesus was able to endure the cross because He saw the joy set before Him. What lies on the other side of the cross (in this life) that you can draw strength from and that will supernaturally enable you to bear your cross with joy?

4. Set aside time today to be God's friend—whatever that looks like for you. Draw near to Him and receive strength from Him. Ask Him to show you the joy that He has set before you so that you can be a lover of the cross.

Surrendering to His Call

I remember the day and place I prayed these words as a young man in the Jesus People movement in the early 1970s: "Here I am, Lord. I sign up to be on the frontlines of what You are doing across the earth. If You are moving, I want in on it! Here I am. I surrender to You, Lord."

I signed my life over to Jesus years ago and have no intention of taking it back. My life is no longer my own. In one sense I am not even looking to reenlist. I am what you call career military. I have been bought with a price and my life is now hidden with Christ in God (see Colossians 3:3). When I search for my life apart from Him, I cannot find it. He took me up on the deal, hid my life in Himself years ago, and any attempt I make to find it elsewhere ends up in a lonely, pathetic side alley.

Often we start out with great zeal mixed with unperceived, zealous ambition propelling us forward to the frontlines of service. God allows this. He even hooks us and draws us in to His purposes. He loves passionate people! He would rather have a piece of rock to chisel than some passive blob.

Another ageless hymn contains the content of what I am attempting to convey. Remember, we surrender first to the Person

and then to the purpose. Let's review the piercing words of "I Surrender All" penned by J. W. Van Deventer in 1896. I encourage you
to read them slowly or sing them if you know this intimate song:

> All to Jesus I surrender,
> All to Him I freely give;
> I will ever love and trust Him,
> In His presence daily live.
>
> [Refrain]
> I surrender all,
> I surrender all,
> All to Thee, my blessed Savior,
> I surrender all.
>
> All to Jesus I surrender,
> Humbly at His feet I bow,
> Worldly pleasures all forsaken,
> Take me, Jesus, take me now.
>
> All to Jesus I surrender,
> Make me, Savior, wholly Thine;
> Let me feel the Holy Spirit,
> Truly know that Thou art mine.
>
> All to Jesus I surrender,
> Lord, I give myself to Thee;
> Fill me with Thy love and power,
> Let Thy blessing fall on me.
>
> All to Jesus I surrender,
> Now I feel the sacred flame;
> Oh, the joy of full salvation!
> Glory, glory to His name!

Guess what? When you read that hymn, I believe you made
it into a prayer. God heard that prayer and will take you up on
it from this day forward.

God's Unfolding Plans

I was called from my mother's womb to help change the spiritual equilibrium of the Church—to unsettle her from her temporary state of lethargy and call forth a generation of passionate, consecrated warriors. Nothing short of a global, prophetic awakening in the Church will ever satisfy my soul, this side of heaven.

Jesus is in charge of our callings and giftings. No person can give you a calling in this life. Gifts are His alone for the giving. A purpose or destiny is His to distribute. The call of when, what and with whom is not about us; it is up to Him.

Ephesians 1:18 spells it out very plainly for us: "I pray that the eyes of your heart may be enlightened, so that you will know what is the hope of His calling." I like that. It is not the hope of *my* calling; it is *His* calling. That sets me free. I do not have to sweat something up. He has a plan, and is more committed to working out that plan than even I am. I then become a steward of the gift, cause, calling or grace of God. I sure want to be a good one.

The ways of God with humankind are a wonder to behold. While biblical principles apply to us all, His ways and means are distinct with each one of His kids. Being a father of four children who are now adults, I have definitely learned that what works with one does not necessarily work with another. There is no cookie-cutter parenting, and it seems that God does no carbon-copying in His approach to us, either. After all, He is a real Father and we really are His individual, "fearfully and wonderfully made" kids.

As with any office or ministry gift, three principles always apply: *called, trained* and *commissioned*. These steps are not just a onetime series of events, but are often repeated several times in an individual's life. Gifts and callings are not stagnant but progressive in nature. Let's consider how God leads us through each of these progressive steps as we surrender our all to His call.

1. The Way God Calls

How does the prophetic call come? As we compare scriptural examples as well as contemporary life experiences, we find a variety of times, styles and ways people have been called into prophetic ministry. Some seem to be born with a gift. Others are born again with a gift, or baptized with the Spirit with a gift. Still other callings are gradual and emerge later in life, even though the person was called sovereignly before he or she was born.

Following are a few biblical examples of people called in diverse ways to prophesy:

Samuel: called as a child (see 1 Samuel 3:1–14)

Elisha: called as a man while plowing a field (see 1 Kings 19:19–21)

Jeremiah: called before he was conceived (see Jeremiah 1:4–19)

Amos: called while he was a herdsman and grower of figs (see Amos 1:1; 7:12–14)

John the Baptist: called in the womb (see Luke 1:41)

How Do I Know If I Am Called?

The next logical question is, What about me? How do I know if I have a specialized prophetic gift or ministry (see 1 Peter 4:10–11)? Here are a few signals to look for in your or another person's life:

- You encounter supernatural events, visitation of angels or Jesus (see 1 Samuel 3:1–14; Isaiah 6:1–13; Jeremiah 1:4–19)
- People begin to tell you (see 1 Samuel 3:9, 20)
- Leadership recognizes it (see Proverbs 18:16)
- You receive an initial prophecy about the future (like Samuel, Isaiah, Jeremiah, Zechariah)

- The gifts of the Spirit through others call you forth (see Acts 13:1–3; 2 Timothy 1:6)
- God confirms His word (see 2 Corinthians 13:1)
- Fruit is produced (see Mark 16:20)

My Own Calling Experience

Even though my mother was never barren, she did miscarry a little boy who had been in her womb five months. She lifted a prayer on that day—July 3, 1951—that God heard. "Lord, if You will give me another son," she said, "I will dedicate him to Christ's service." One year later, to the exact date, my parents were overjoyed to greet their third child and only son into the world in a home birth.

I think I must have come out of the womb waving my hands and shouting, "Hallelujah!" All I have ever known in this life is Jesus. All I have ever wanted to do is know and love Him. He is my passion. Apart from Him I have no breath, no meaning, no life.

As I grew up it seemed that I was kept on a short leash. I could not do the things a lot of kids did. One reason was the haunting prayers of my mother. The youngest of four children, she had parents who feared the Lord—the "give-me-that-old-time-religion" kind of stuff. Her brother, my uncle Arnold, after celebrating his ninetieth birthday, departed to his heavenly reward. He had served in the United Methodist ministry more than sixty years. Many felt that I was pegged to follow in his footsteps.

I remember as a child sitting at the feet of Great-Grandmother Hall's rocking chair. This country, hardworking lady—my dad's grandmother—looked down at me and said something like this: "He has a good, straight back. He'll make a good preacher someday." I also recall my eighth-grade teacher, who said, "He'll either be a preacher or a lawyer. He can argue with a fencepost and win!" I do not know if they were prophesying or not. All I know is, I remember what they said and it stuck with me.

Years passed with many wonderful experiences with God, church and long walks on which I poured my heart out to the Lover of my soul. Then, around the age of twenty, I ran square-dab into the Jesus People movement. It was as though I instantly found home, destiny and purpose. Gifts exploded as I became filled with the Holy Spirit. I started prophesying then and have never stopped.

Thereafter, for the next ten years, I prayed almost daily for the school of the prophets to come forth, like the school under the prophet Samuel (see 1 Samuel 19:20). I really did not know what I was asking for. All I knew was that as I delighted myself in Jesus, He put His desires for my life into my heart. My heart was now beating in unison with His. And remember, when two hearts beat as one, heaven's ladder will come down.

I could tell you many wonderful stories, but the truth is, prophesying is *His* calling. Not mine, not yours. When you try in your own strength to bring something into being, it is frustrating at best; but when He is your primary focus, you both will succeed.

2. Getting Your Training Wheels

Have you ever encountered someone who has been given his or her prophetic driver's license without having gone through driver's education classes? To use another illustration, some folks are trying to perform advanced techniques in public pro-phetic acrobatics when they have not even had experience on the practice mat in their local church. Help, Lord! And, yes, He is coming to our aid.

When I began more than 35 years ago, there were no classes to attend, no schools of the Spirit that I knew of, no national prophetic conferences. I *eventually* had two books as my mentors—the classic book *The Elijah Task* by the faithful pioneers John and Paula Sandford and the excellent training manual *Interpreting Symbols and Types* from the brilliant teaching ministry of Kevin Conner. Today many good materials are available and a new generation of fathers and mothers in the prophetic has emerged.

Training opportunities today abound. Take advantage of them! Get out there on the practice mat, align yourself with a team of believers or a specialized ministry and exercise your gifts. Learn to drive the proper way, for Jesus' sake.

How Are Spiritual Gifts Received?

You may have heard the statement "gifts are given and fruit is grown." How *are* gifts given? How does increase come? As one of the fathers in the prophetic movement today, let me give you a simple word. These precious prophetic graces are the activity of the Holy Spirit as a result of our personal calling and are cultivated by a relationship with Him. We can only teach you how to yield to the activity of the Spirit, and how not to conjure up an imitation.

Although each of us is unique, some basic principles apply to all of us. Thus, just as we can learn to hear God's voice more effectively, so we can learn to be more open to His gifting. Here are five principles to help us understand how gifts are received and to open our hearts to receiving them.

1. *Gifts are given by a sovereign God.* He gives grace, ministries and offices entirely as He pleases. These gifts may have little or nothing to do with the condition of the person. Acts 2:1–4 and 10:44–46, for instance, tell about vast numbers coming to faith and receiving the gift of tongues at Pentecost, and the results of Peter's preaching to the Gentiles at Cornelius's house.

2. *Gifts are often conveyed by the laying on of hands.* An early example is the gift of wisdom given to Joshua when Moses laid his hands on him (see Deuteronomy 34:9). Another is the impartation to Saul of the gift of the Holy Spirit and the return of his sight when Ananias laid hands on him (see Acts 9:17–18). People are often equipped for ministry by the laying on of hands, like the seven men chosen to oversee the daily serving of food in the early Church (see Acts 6:3–6) and Barnabas and Saul before being sent out by the church at Antioch (see Acts 13:1–3). This practice is to be used advisedly, however. Paul warns Timothy not to be hasty about laying hands on others for gifting lest he "share responsibility for the sins of others" (1 Timothy 5:22).

3. *Gifts can be enhanced through mentoring relationships.* The most noted example is that of Jesus and His disciples. The Lord called the Twelve and passed on His authority (see Luke 10:1–11, 19). Another prominent example is Elijah's anointing of Elisha, who followed his master through years of training and service. Recall that when Elijah was taken into heaven, Elisha took up the older prophet's mantle and began his own ministry (see 1 Kings 19:15–21; 2 Kings 2:1–15).

4. *Gifts we have already received can be developed further.* We should mature in and grow more sensitive to the gifts we have already received from God. Hebrews 5:14 tells us to practice and train our senses in order to mature. Ways to do this include prayer, fasting, self-restraint, increasing in faith, growing in character and holding to orthodox doctrine.

5. *Gifts come from God only by grace.* Self-righteousness is a serious hindrance to the development of gifts. Gifts are gifts! They do not prove how much God loves or wants to favor the prophet or teacher or evangelist; rather, they show how much God loves and wants to bless the people.

A Grace That Had Evaded Me

Many years ago I just plain could not teach. I could share from my heart, but I did not have a natural propensity toward teaching. At that time my primary mentors and peers were all gifted teachers. I felt like a fish out of water most of the time. I had the heart of a shepherd with a budding call of a prophet, but a teacher I was not.

Then, at a small group meeting one night, a young co-leader with me in the Jesus People movement approached me. "I feel the Lord is saying that you are to ask for any gift that you want," he said, "and God will give it to you."

It seemed a bit unusual, yet I knew this was the voice of my Master speaking. I pondered for a bit, then responded by expressing the desire for the grace to teach God's people.

My friend laid his hands on me and quietly prayed for me. Something happened—two things, to be exact.

First, as I wondered why I had not asked for the gift of miracles or evangelism or something more dramatic, faith rose up in my heart and I knew I had asked for the very thing God wanted me to receive. Second, after my friend prayed, I was different. I was not sure how, but I knew I had received a grace that had previously evaded me. I asked for a gift of teaching.

3. Commissioning—Getting Your Driver's License

Your life and ministry can see many progressive commissionings and appointments. We are called and we continue to be called. We are trained and we continue to be trained. We are sent out and we are brought back again to be retrained, retooled and given a new vision, so that we can be recommissioned with fresh purpose and power. What are some of the signs that a commissioning has been or is being granted by God (who alone can do it)?

1. God backs up the words; they do not fail.

2. People recognize the power, accuracy and consistency.

3. The Lord appears to the individual through various means.

4. The word of the Lord comes to the prophetic person more consistently.

There is another sign of a commissioning, too; it is called the sign of "da boot"! If you wait around too long expecting perfection of character before any commissioning comes, then you might be in for a rude awakening. Yes, you might just get a kick in the seat of your pants, and God might have to say, "Well, do something with what you've got, and then I'll give you more!" Or He might say, "Have you obeyed My last orders?" You respond, a bit puzzled, "What orders, exactly, have I received?" And He responds with His Word, reminding us, "I have already said, 'Go, therefore.'"

So my counsel to you is, *Get to gettin'!* Get into your vehicle and start the ignition.

There is a cave of preparation for every prophetic person. Sometimes it seems that the Holy Spirit is whispering, "Come out, come out, wherever you are." If ever there was a time to report for duty, it is today. Stand up and be counted. Are you ready to report for service?

A Lifestyle of Intimacy Is Yours to Live

As with John and the other disciples, Jesus calls us to follow Him—to embrace an intimate walk with Him down a narrow road. An intimate invitation is how Christ calls us, it is how we walk with Him, and it is what we are living for—to see Him face-to-face and be with Him forever.

In this section on the lifestyle of intimacy, we began by looking at John the Beloved, the intimate friendship He had with

Jesus and God's desire to breathe upon us as carriers of His awesome presence. We recognized some leaves we hide behind and emphasized the importance of coming into the light. We saw that even those who are pursuing intimacy with Jesus must be alert in the Spirit and cultivate authentic character in Christ. Being a friend of God and loving the cross is truly a precious journey that has unspeakable joys waiting for us on the road ahead. Lastly we examined how to surrender to God's call. Have you surrendered? Will you surrender afresh to Jesus right now?

⟩ P R A Y E R ⟨

King Jesus, You are the great God of heaven and earth. From You, through You and to You are all things. You are fully in charge and I acknowledge Your Lordship over my life. Right now I surrender fully to You to follow You faithfully all my days. You are a glorious and majestic leader. Lead me by Your grace into a deeper lifestyle of intimacy. Thank You for calling me into such a precious salvation. You are faithful and will surely bring to pass all that You have spoken. Here I am reporting for service. Use me. Train me. Be my teacher. Send me forth for Your holy name's sake. Amen.

Embracing Your Calling—Day 7

1. How were you called by God? What signs have confirmed His calling on your life?

2. What do you do when the enemy questions your calling through condemning thoughts, criticism, accusation, etc.?

3. From the "How Are Spiritual Gifts Received?" section, which one of the five ways best describes how you got your "training wheels"?

4. Pause right now, go back to the first part of this day's reading and sing "I Surrender All." Make it your prayer. Make it your life.

The Lifestyle of Wisdom

Behold, You desire truth in the innermost being, and
in the hidden part You will make me know wisdom.

PSALM 51:6

Joseph—Prophet
of Learned Wisdom

Joseph is truly one of the most remarkable characters in the Bible. The book of Genesis devotes fourteen chapters to his life from his teenage years until his death at 110. We can learn many valuable lessons from the life of Joseph as he walked into the destiny God designed for him.

As we begin this section on "The Lifestyle of Wisdom," let's take a moment to look at this prophet of learned wisdom. Did you catch that? *Learned* wisdom. Joseph did not start off as a leader wisely storing up food during years of plenty to save the world from famine. He could hardly lead himself, and he certainly was not ready to govern Egypt. But Joseph learned wisdom. What he learned saved his family and all of Egypt from starvation and set the stage for the nation of Israel to grow from seventy to more than one million people.

What is your destiny and how will you seize it in God? You can be sure it will require learned wisdom.

Dreams and a Lack of Wisdom

At the age of seventeen the favored son of Jacob had a dream from the Lord. Joseph responded to the revelation, zealously and ignorantly, by sharing it with his brothers, thinking they would be as thrilled about it as he was. "Please listen to this dream which I have had; for behold, we were binding sheaves in the field, and lo, my sheaf rose up and also stood erect; and behold, your sheaves gathered around and bowed down to my sheaf" (Genesis 37:6–7). Joseph's brothers were already jealous of him because their father had singled him out and given him that special coat of many colors. But when Joseph shared what was spoken to him privately by God, his brothers hated him even more.

At this stage of his life, Joseph had not developed much wisdom. Wisdom is not a gift (although a "word of wisdom" is). It must be developed and gained through teaching and experience. Joseph apparently lacked both.

Then he shared another dream indicating that even his father and mother would bow down to him. The whole family was aghast at this audacious dream, and he began to suffer severe persecution. Guess what? Persecution sometimes follows people of vision. Misunderstanding and jealousy often come with the territory, whether or not you are wise.

Joseph became the target of an evil plot devised by his brothers. They threw him into a pit, thinking to murder him, but instead sold him to Midianite traders, and he was taken to Egypt. At that point it did not look as if anybody was going to bow down to Joseph. It looked as though Joseph was doing all the bowing!

More Dreams and Learning Wisdom

After Joseph arrived in Egypt, he was sold into slavery and brought into the service of Potiphar, an Egyptian officer of

Pharaoh. But the Lord was with Joseph and he found favor with his master. "So [Potiphar] left everything he owned in Joseph's charge; and with him there he did not concern himself with anything except the food which he ate" (Genesis 39:6).

Things did not stay rosy for long. Potiphar's manipulative wife unjustly accused Joseph of taking advantage of her after he refused her advances. This time, although Joseph was walking in wisdom, he was persecuted again. Off to prison he went. But even there the Lord was with Joseph, and he found favor with the jailer. "The chief jailer did not supervise anything under Joseph's charge because the LORD was with him; and whatever he did, the LORD made to prosper" (Genesis 39:23).

Think of the discouragement Joseph must have faced in the darkness of the dungeon. He had finally gotten to a place of significance and honor in his life, and *wham!* More injustice, and he found himself in jail with some pretty rough characters.

But God did an awesome thing with Joseph in the midst of that hopeless-looking set of circumstances. While the Hebrew was seemingly wasting away in an Egyptian prison, God began to deepen his revelatory gifting, and he interpreted two other prisoners' dreams. As he practiced his gifting on these fellow inmates, his reputation within the prison grew. Eventually Pharaoh heard about the amazing young prisoner who could interpret dreams with astounding accuracy. Pharaoh called Joseph out of prison to help him with a set of perplexing dreams. None of Pharaoh's wise men and magicians had been able to interpret them, so out of desperation he turned to the Hebrew for answers.

After skillfully interpreting Pharaoh's dreams and giving credit to the Lord, Joseph proceeded to give Pharaoh an action plan to prepare Egypt for the famine predicted in the dreams. Action must follow vision.

Joseph had learned well in the difficult place of trial and testing. He dreamed, interpreted, then implemented the dreams of God, and he was again promoted to a place of authority. Pharaoh declared, "See, I have set you over all the land of Egypt" (Genesis 41:41). God used what seemed like a nightmare to Joseph in order to prepare him for the manifestation of his own dream.

From Dreamer to Deliverer

Joseph was a man who had literally been brought out of the pit into a place of prominence, respect and authority. God's favor surrounded him and caused him and a whole nation to prosper, even in a time of famine. God did amazing things in and through Joseph, and continued to work out the dreams He had originally placed in Joseph's heart.

Because of severe famine that spread beyond the borders of Egypt into Canaan, Joseph's brothers came to Egypt seeking food that had been made available by the hand of God. Eventually Joseph revealed himself to his brothers, who had violated him horribly. Joseph stated with a forgiving heart, "God sent me before you to preserve for you a remnant in the earth, and to keep you alive by a great deliverance" (Genesis 45:7). This wisdom revelation is summed up in Genesis 50:20: "As for you, you meant evil against me, but God meant it for good in order to bring about this present result, to preserve many people alive."

God took a proud and haughty young dreamer and turned him into a man who carried the humility, wisdom and skill of his God. He dared to dream God's dreams, and God changed him into a deliverer.

Lessons to Learn from Joseph

Look at the lessons we can learn from Joseph:

Joseph did not know the proper ways of responding to revelation.

Genesis 37:3–4 records that Joseph's brothers knew that their father, Jacob, preferred Joseph and loved him more than all his sons. The Bible says that "they hated him and could not speak to him on friendly terms." Do you think Joseph knew his brothers did not like him? If they could not speak to him on friendly terms, you would figure Joseph had some idea that he was not liked or appreciated.

Yet immediately following his dream, what was Joseph thinking? *I'm going to go tell my brothers who already hate me and treat me poorly about my dream foretelling that I am going to rule over them, even though I am younger than all of them.* I honestly do not think Joseph was spiteful or was trying to rub it in. I think he was not thinking what might happen. So his brothers "hated him even more for his dreams and for his words" (verse 8).

So the intensity increased against Joseph, but what did Joseph do the next time he had a dream? He immediately went and told it to his brothers! Seriously? You would assume he would have gained some wisdom from the last time he shared his dream. But he had not. Even his father rebuked him (see verse 10).

Proverbs 14:33 suggests we must first ask permission to tell our revelation: "Wisdom rests quietly in the heart of him who has understanding, but what is in the heart of fools is made known" (NKJV). Others might not have the wisdom and maturity to handle the repercussions of the words we bring. Joseph's brothers certainly did not. I wonder what might have happened if Joseph had prayed before speaking about his dreams. The key to remember is to *pray before you act*! Prayer should always be your first act in response to revelation.

Joseph learned wisdom through his failures.

Genesis 40:8 reveals that Joseph learned to seek the wisdom of God in order to interpret his revelations properly. Upon observing the sad faces of the cupbearer and the baker and then learning the cause was a dream, Joseph said confidently: "Do not interpretations belong to God? Tell it to me, please." He easily and accurately interpreted both dreams, which turned out to be the key to his release from jail.

When Joseph was brought before Pharaoh to interpret his dream, Pharaoh said, "I have heard it said about you, that when you hear a dream you can interpret it." Joseph's answered Pharaoh with this response: "It is not in me; God will give Pharaoh a favorable answer (Genesis 41:15–16). Clearly Joseph was the star of the show here. He had correctly interpreted the butler's and baker's dreams, and now the ruler of Egypt was calling upon a Hebrew slave to bring understanding to a troubling dream. Yet Joseph made it known that his God would provide not just an interpretation, but a *favorable* answer. Joseph had come a long way from being seventeen and green in prophetic wisdom.

Joseph showed that the right attitude would keep him going in the right direction.

Have you ever noticed that Joseph's character was impeccable while in captivity? He turned away from the advances of Potiphar's wife. There is no record of Joseph complaining after he was falsely accused and put into prison. (If you have not noticed, the Bible is not shy about exposing breaches of character. If Joseph had complained, the Bible would have recorded it.) Instead, we learn that Joseph found favor with the chief jailer who put Joseph in charge of the prison. Joseph was respectful and kind. This attitude was visible to all, and it released favor from those in authority.

How about when Joseph's brothers showed up on the scene? Although Joseph tested them, as commander over all of Egypt he easily could have made their lives quite difficult. And why not after all the suffering they caused him and their father, Jacob. But what was Joseph's response when he saw his brothers? Rage? Unforgiveness? No, he wept. Be careful not to harden yourself against your gift and calling. Do not curse your sensitivity; rather, embrace it and let it make you, like Joseph, one who weeps over his brothers.

Also look at Joseph's attitude after Jacob had died when he could have taken vengeance on his brothers if there was any residue of bitterness left in his heart: "Do not be afraid, for am I in God's place? As for you, you meant evil against me, but God meant it for good in order to bring about this present result, to preserve many people alive. So therefore, do not be afraid; I will provide for you and your little ones." To conclude their time together, Joseph "comforted them and spoke kindly to them" (Genesis 50:19–21).

Is this amazing? Joseph intentionally set his heart toward the Lord when he entered Egypt as a slave at seventeen where it remained until his death at 110. The result benefited not only him, but also the superpower nation of that day, surrounding countries and, maybe more significantly, a group of seventy sheep farmers who were to become a nation from which the Messiah would come.

Today God is looking for those who will embrace the cross of the prophetic lifestyle and be vessels who will carry the prophetic message, instead of being crushed by it. The apostle Paul, who also experienced undeserved hardship, exhorted the Philippians:

> Have this attitude in yourselves which was also in Christ Jesus, who, although He existed in the form of God, did not regard equality with God a thing to be grasped, but emptied Himself, taking the form of a bond-servant, and being made in the likeness

of men. Being found in appearance as a man, He humbled Himself by becoming obedient to the point of death, even death on a cross. For this reason also, God highly exalted Him.

Philippians 2:5–9

So do not lose heart. Just like Joseph, you, too, "in due time will reap if [you] do not grow weary" (Galatians 6:9).

Joseph did not let go of his dreams until he saw them come to fruition.

The manifestation of your revelation will take time. Joseph was seventeen when he first dreamed. He was thirty years old when Pharaoh put Egypt under his rule. And it was another nine years before he would see his brothers bow before him like the sheaves in his dream. There is nothing quite like waiting more than twenty years for a dream to come true. But in one day he went from being a prisoner to being married to Pharaoh's daughter and ruler over all of Egypt. In a few months he went from being an orphan alone in a strange land to having his father and brothers joining him in Egypt.

If you have been waiting on a dream or revelation for a few months or many years, do not let it go. "Faithful is He who calls you, and He also will bring it to pass" (1 Thessalonians 5:24).

Lifestyle of Wisdom

When Pharaoh was looking for a solution to the problem his dream revealed, he said to Joseph, "There is no one as discerning and wise as you are" (Genesis 41:39). That is quite a statement considering he was the ruler of Egypt and had at his disposal the wisdom and resources of his vast land. I believe that what he saw in Joseph was not just a lucky guess about a bad dream, but a lifestyle of discernment and wisdom into which Pharaoh could entrust the well-being of Egypt.

The next six readings in this section are focused on aspects of a lifestyle of wisdom. Proverbs is peppered with admonitions about wisdom and the importance to acquire it. Here are just a few:

Proverbs 2:2—"Make your ear attentive to wisdom."

Proverbs 4:5—"Acquire wisdom!"

Proverbs 16:16—"How much better it is to get wisdom than gold!"

Proverbs 19:8—"He who gets wisdom loves his own soul."

Proverbs 23:23—"Get wisdom and instruction and understanding."

Psalm 51:6 declares, "Behold, You desire truth in the innermost being, and in the hidden part You will make me know wisdom." *Yes, Lord, make us to know wisdom so that we can demonstrate a lifestyle of the wisdom as we use the glorious storehouse of revelation You give us to make Christ known.* As you conclude each reading in this section, I encourage you to cry out to God for the wisdom from above that He promises to give in generous amounts to all who ask (see James 1:5). So ask and He will give generously.

⟩ P R A Y E R ⟨

Yes, Lord, I confess that I lack the wisdom I need to live a life worthy of the calling I have received from You. So I ask You for Your eternal wisdom from above—wisdom to respond rightly to the revelation You give to me; wisdom to learn through my mistakes; wisdom to keep my attitude in the right place when I just want to complain; wisdom to hold on to my dreams until I see them come to pass. You are amazing, Jesus. Now unto the King eternal, immortal, invisible—to God who alone is wise—be honor and glory forever and ever. Amen.

⬛ Embracing Your Calling—Day 8

1. What dreams or visions has God given to you that you have not yet seen come to pass?

2. Have you stepped out to share revelation the Lord has given to you only to have that revelation met with disbelief or criticism like Joseph? What happened and how did you respond?

3. What favor have you found with God and others during "prison" assignments that have come your way?

4. No matter where you are on your prophetic journey, take a step back and ask God to show you your life from His perspective. Joseph did not know that he was destined for the palace, yet he was faithful and honored the Lord. As a result he was fully prepared for the palace. Talk to Jesus about your desire to be faithful to Him no matter what.

Our Revelatory Storehouse

Through wisdom Joseph built storehouses to hold grain that would be distributed throughout Egypt and the surrounding countries during the years of severe famine. In the same way, God has also provided a storehouse of revelation to those who, through wisdom, will seek these prophetic riches and share them with others.

The following foundational Scripture holds three keys to receiving and releasing the gift of prophecy.

> Earnestly desire and zealously cultivate the greatest and best— the higher [gifts] and the choicest [graces]. And yet I will show you a still more excellent way—one that is better by far and the highest of them all, [love].
>
> 1 Corinthians 12:31, AMP

The first key: *We must remind ourselves that revelation from God is a gift*. You and I cannot earn that gift; it is given freely to any who are hungry.

Once as I was sitting at my desk, doing nothing in particular, not even earnestly seeking God, the voice of the Lord resounded within me. He said simply, *You are now hearing Me through a gift.*

We are not *qualified* to receive, but we are *able* to receive because of the unmerited riches of His grace that have been freely bestowed on us through the sacrifice of Christ, through the power of the Spirit. Prophetic revelation is a present from the heart of the Father. We can situate ourselves in such a manner as to cooperate with His grace, but we cannot earn it. When a word from God comes to us as we minister to others, we are hearing Him through a gift—God's grace. This puts us all on level ground.

God wants us to hear His voice even more than we want to hear it. And the way we hear Him is through a relationship. This is the second key to receiving the gift of prophecy: *We must cultivate a love relationship with the Father God.* We hear Him when we pray. We hear Him by reading His written Word. We hear Him because we are sons and daughters in relationship with our awesome Father. No gifting can ever take the place of a relationship. A love relationship with our Father God through Jesus Christ is the foundation of all true communion. Remember the words from the old hymn, *And He walks with me, and He talks with me.*

Paul's admonition to the church at Corinth to "pursue love, yet earnestly desire the spiritual gifts, but especially that you may prophesy" (1 Corinthians 14:1) was written not to a select group of people or only to those holding the office of prophet, but to the everyday believer at Corinth—and to you and me. The target: the character of Christ. Paul wanted their storehouses filled with love (see 1 Corinthians 13), yet he still urged them to *earnestly desire!* This is the third key.

The word *desire* means to have a deep-seated yearning for something. It is not wrong to want, desire and crave the operation of the gifts of the Spirit in your life. In fact, the Church is exhorted by the Lord through Paul to pursue these passionately.

Our Father wants us filled with His love and the gifts of His Spirit so His people are not without vision and encouragement.

With ravenous hunger, then, pursue the transforming grace packages of God so that His love will leave an unforgettable mark on the heart of another. Fan into flame your craving, your longing, your desire for the gifts and graces of God. Use this third key of passionate desire to receive and release the gifts of revelation, so that you may build up, exhort and bring comfort to many needy souls as you aim for the character of Christ.

What Is the Gift of Prophecy?

Holding these three important keys, we can go on to define the gift of prophecy. We begin with definitions from noted teachers who have emerged from different moves of the Spirit of God— the healing revival, the Latter Rain movement, the charismatic renewal, the Pentecostal tradition, the liturgical Church and the perspective of the Third Wave. As we look at these definitions, we find that each has a particular slant. When we combine the definitions, we come up with an excellent composite picture of the gift of prophecy.

Let's lay the pieces out on the table to see the greater whole.

Prophecy is supernatural utterance in a known tongue. The Hebrew word for *prophesy* means "to flow forth." It also carries with it the thought "to bubble forth like a fountain, to let drop, to lift up, to tumble forth, and to spring forth." The Greek word translated "to prophesy" means "to speak for another." *It means to speak for God or to be His spokesman.*[1]

Kenneth Hagin
Late father of the Faith Movement

The gift of prophecy is speaking under the direct supernatural influence of the Holy Spirit. It is becoming God's mouthpiece, verbalizing His words as the Spirit directs. The Greek word *propheteia* means "speaking forth the mind and counsel of God." It is inseparable in its New Testament usage from the concept of the direct inspiration of the Spirit. *Prophecy is the very voice of Christ speaking in the Church.*[2]

Dick Iverson
Apostolic leader of Ministers
Fellowship International

The gift of prophecy is the supernaturally imparted ability to hear the voice of the Holy Spirit and to speak God's mind or counsel. Prophecy ministers not only to the assembled group of believers but to individuals. Its three main purposes:

1. *To edify:* build up, strengthen, make more effective
2. *To exhort:* stimulate, encourage, admonish
3. *To comfort:* cheer up

Thus prophecy overcomes two of Satan's most common attacks: condemnation and discouragement.[3]

Derek Prince
Late international Bible
teacher, author

New Testament prophecy occurs when a Spirit-filled Christian receives a "revelation" (*apokaupsis*) from God and then declares that revelation to the gathered Church under the impetus of the Holy Spirit. Such revelation enables the Church to know something from the perspective of the Kingdom of God. The essential makeup of a prophecy is fivefold:

- God gives a revelation (communication, divine truth, message, insight)
- to a Spirit-filled Christian (one of God's people, a spiritual intermediary)
- who speaks it forth (an oral declaration)
- to the gathered Church (the public assembly of believers)

- under the impetus (inspiration, stimulation, prompting, encouragement, empowerment) of the Holy Spirit[4]

Ernest Gentile
Author, preacher, prophet

The Greek *propheteia*, according to Vine's *Expository Dictionary of New Testament Words,* is a noun that "signifies the speaking forth the mind and counsel of God. It is the declaration of that which cannot be known by natural means. It is the forth-telling of the will of God, whether with reference to the past, the present, or the future." New Testament prophecy functions in three realms:

1. Jesus giving inspired testimony and praise through one of His saints by prophetic utterance or song of the Lord (Hebrews 2:12; Revelation 19:10)
2. One of the manifestations of the Holy Spirit called the gift of prophecy that brings edification, exhortation and comfort to the Body of Christ (Romans 12:6; 1 Corinthians 12:10)
3. The prophet speaking by divine utterance the mind and counsel of God and giving a *rhema* word for edification, direction, correction, confirmation and instruction in righteousness (1 Corinthians 14:29; 2 Timothy 3:16–17)

A divinely inspired prophecy is the Holy Spirit expressing the thoughts and desires of Christ through a human voice.[5]

Bill Hamon
Founder of Christian International,
apostolic prophet, author

The gift of prophecy is the special ability God gives to a certain member of the Body of Christ to receive and communicate an immediate message of God to His people through a divinely anointed utterance (Luke 7:26; Acts 15:32; 21:9–11; Romans 12:6; 1 Corinthians 12:10, 28; Ephesians 4:11–14).[6]

C. Peter Wagner
Author, chancellor of Wagner Leadership Institute

The Gift of Prophecy versus the Office of a Prophet

What, then, is prophecy? We could say that prophecy is the expressed thoughts of God spoken in a language that no person in his or her natural gift of speech could ever articulate. The substance and nature of prophecy exceed the limits of what the natural mind can conceive. God's thoughts are not our thoughts (see Isaiah 55:8). The gift of prophecy may come through human mouths or actions, but it originates in the mind of God—spiritual thoughts in spiritual words and demonstrations (see 1 Corinthians 2:9–16).

In this hour we must learn to distinguish among the gifts and offices of the Spirit. While they are from the same Lord and Spirit, and their functions overlap, we must yet acknowledge the distinctions so as not to act presumptuously in their outworking. Not all who prophesy are prophets. Not all authentic prophets speak and address the same spheres of life and ministry. We need clarification in this foundational area to help maintain our proper spiritual equilibrium.

Following is a brief comparison that I adapted from some of the early teachings of John Paul Jackson, author and director of Streams Ministries:

Gifts of the Holy Spirit	Ministry or Office Gifts
Given by the Spirit (see 1 Corinthians 12; 14)	Given by Jesus (see Ephesians 4)
If prophecy, given to all (see 1 Corinthians 14:24, 31)	If prophecy, given to some (see Ephesians 4:11; 1 Corinthians 12:29)
Given for edification, exhortation, comfort (see 1 Corinthians 14:3)	Same, plus correction and direction
Given to the Body for the common good (see 1 Corinthians 12:7)	Given to lay the foundation of the Church and lead and equip the people (Ephesians 2:20; 4:12)
Given to the members of the Body (see 1 Corinthians 12:12)	Act as joints, holding the Body members together (see Ephesians 4:16)

Gifts of the Holy Spirit	Ministry or Office Gifts
Involve revelations of the past and present (see 1 Corinthians 12:8–10)	Involve revelations of the past, present and future (see Acts 11:28; 21:10–11)
Speak primarily to the Body (see 1 Corinthians 12:14–26)	Speak to the Body and also to the nations (see Acts 21:10; Jeremiah 1:5, 10)
Deliver the Word (see 1 Corinthians 14:12)	Become the Word (Agabus, Isaiah, Hosea)
Speak to the Church (see 1 Corinthians 14:2–4)	Speak to the past, present and future Church, and to social, political, economic and geological arenas (Nahum, Hosea, Obadiah, Elijah, Daniel, Agabus)
Involve intercession to make the desires of the people known to God	Involve prophecy to make the desires of God known to the people
Speak of God's grace	Speak of God's grace and judgment

This is but an overview in the vast storehouse of the study of prophecy. Stay with me.

Present Purposes of Prophecy

The gift of prophecy is like Jesus standing up inside a person, waving His hand and saying, "I have something encouraging I want to bring to you, My people. I have a word of comfort. I have a word of edification. I have a word of learning." The gift of prophecy is the testimony of Jesus that will motivate us to persevere and to pray. In other words, Jesus has something to say.

Jesus promised that the Holy Spirit would speak to us about the things that are to come (see John 16:13). Why? To prepare us for those events ahead of time. The gift of prophecy brings hope and the restoration of faith for the days ahead. It sheds light on our sometimes dark path.

Following is a scriptural list of some of the present-day purposes of this wonderful gift.

1. *Edification.* "Pursue love, yet desire earnestly spiritual gifts, but especially that you may prophesy" (1 Corinthians 14:1). God has provided this gift to edify or build up the Church (see 1 Corinthians 3:10–15; 14:2–4).

2. *Exhortation.* God wants us to incite, encourage, advise and warn earnestly (see Hosea 6:1–3; 1 Corinthians 14:3; 1 Timothy 4). Prod others on to love and good deeds by exhorting them.

3. *Comfort.* When this occurs, it is Christ speaking in great personal concern, tenderness and care to release the comfort of His presence in times of need (see 1 Corinthians 14:3). Ever need comfort? You will reap what you sow!

4. *Conviction and convincing.* "If all prophesy, and an unbeliever or an ungifted man enters, he is convicted by all, he is called to account by all; the secrets of his heart are disclosed; and so he will fall on his face and worship God, declaring that God is certainly among you" (1 Corinthians 14:24–25). This relates to believers who are unlearned and uninitiated in the present-day operation of the gifts of the Holy Spirit, as well as unbelievers who have yet to come to the saving knowledge of our Lord. Here the prophetic is also used to convict us, to prick our consciences concerning sin, but with a heart to bring about repentance and reconciliation.

5. *Instruction and learning.* "You can all prophesy one by one, so that all may learn and all may be exhorted" (1 Corinthians 14:31). As the revelatory gifts open the Scriptures to us, great truth is seen and new understanding opened up.

6. *Gift impartation.* "Do not neglect the spiritual gift within you, which was bestowed on you through prophetic utterance with the laying on of hands by the presbytery. Take pains with these things; be absorbed in them, so that your progress will be evident to all" (1 Timothy 4:14–15). We

are not to disregard the gifts that reside within us, especially prophecy. As mentioned in these verses, giftings and callings may be discerned, confirmed or even imparted. Put jumper cables onto the battery of someone's heart and charge him or her up, for Jesus' sake! Give that person a boost to go on to the next level.

7. *Testimony of and from Jesus.* "Then I fell at his feet to worship him. But he said to me, 'Do not do that; I am a fellow servant of yours and your brethren who hold the testimony of Jesus; worship God. For the testimony of Jesus is the spirit of prophecy'" (Revelation 19:10). Jesus stands in the midst of His people to tell of His works. One of the ways He does this is through the present-day operation of the gift of prophecy. When His heart is shared, people realize the Lord is near and not far off, and the hearer is drawn closer to Him.

Examples of the Gift of Prophecy

In the Scriptures prophetic gifting was not reserved for the elite, but was given by the Spirit to those in need of encouragement, instruction, impartation and the testimony of Jesus. Nor was respect given to the maturity of the recipient. Seasoned disciples as well as new converts were used in the gift of prophecy. The common denominator: All were seekers and followers of Christ. The gift was given freely to reveal a loving God who enjoys sharing His heart with His people and who wants to make them increasingly aware of His attentive presence in their lives.

The following Scriptures give us examples of the gift of prophecy operating in and through believers in the New Testament:

Luke 1:66–67: "All who heard them kept them in mind, saying, 'What then will this child turn out to be?' For the hand of the Lord was certainly with him. And his father Zacharias was filled with the Holy Spirit, and prophesied." Zacharias began prophesying concerning the birth of his son, John. A measure of the purposes of God was revealed through this prophetic utterance. This was the experience Michal Ann and I had concerning the births of our four children. By grace the Holy Spirit signified through dreams and visions and revelatory utterances the names and callings of each of them.

Acts 13:2: "While they were ministering to the Lord and fasting, the Holy Spirit said, 'Set apart for Me Barnabas and Saul for the work to which I have called them.'" A directive word of wisdom was given to Barnabas and Saul and the others, apparently through prophecy, while they ministered to the Lord with prayer and fasting.

Acts 19:6: "When Paul had laid his hands upon them, the Holy Spirit came on them, and they began speaking with tongues and prophesying." At times prophecy is one of the signs of the Spirit's overflowing presence in the life of a new believer, as it was for these Ephesians. This is the way it worked with me, too. Before I was ever released into the gift of tongues, I first bubbled up and started speaking God's plan of a great end-time revival covering the earth.

Acts 20:23; 21:4, 11: "'The Holy Spirit solemnly testifies to me in every city, saying that bonds and afflictions await me.' . . . And they kept telling Paul through the Spirit not to set foot in Jerusalem. . . . 'The Holy Spirit says: "In this way the Jews at Jerusalem will bind the man who owns this belt and deliver him into the hands of the Gentiles."'" Prophecy and other ministries apparently combined to give Paul warnings and direction. The apostle was made aware of the cost that confronted him as a result of his interaction with the prophetic. May true, non-judgmental warnings be released to us as well, to prepare us for life's journey.

1 Timothy 1:18: "This command I entrust to you, Timothy, my son, in accordance with the prophecies previously made concerning you, that by them you fight the good fight." Prophecies were used to reveal Timothy's appointed ministry calling, and later to strengthen him in fulfilling that ministry. In Timothy's experience, prophecy was used by the presbytery with laying on of hands for a commissioning of a gift or ministry. This model was restored through the Latter Rain movement of the late 1940s and early 1950s.

Open the Storehouse

What a bountiful, revelatory storehouse God has provided! Remember, however, that Joseph stored up grain to share with the world, not just the Egyptians. Most accounts in Scripture in which the gifts flowed took place when believers sought out non-believers—not simply inviting them into their nice church world, but visiting them where they lived. Jesus commanded us to go, so let's go, but let us go with wisdom.

Next we will look at prophetic ways of wisdom that will help us distribute the Bread of Life most effectively to those who will receive.

=====⟩ P R A Y E R ⟨=====

Jesus, I worship and honor You. You are my storehouse of revelation, encouragement and life. I earnestly desire You and the gifts You want to give to me so that I can be effective for Your Kingdom's sake. Fill me afresh with Your Spirit of wisdom and revelation. Open my heart to know Your heart of love for the world You came to save. Come, Lord Jesus, and stand up inside of me. Speak, encourage, exhort, comfort, instruct, impart and, most of all, testify of Your glory. Amen.

☰ Embracing Your Calling—Day 9

1. What gifts have you received from the Lord? Do you ever find yourself thinking you earned them by demonstrating good character or through good works?

2. How would you define the gift of prophecy?

3. Which of the seven "Present Purposes of Prophecy" do you relate to most or see manifest most frequently in your life? Why?

4. God wants you to hear His voice, and the way you hear it is through a relationship with Father God through Jesus Christ. Take a moment to sit quietly before Him, reflecting upon His love for you and your love for Him. Then ask (according to Ephesians 3:16–19) that you would be rooted and grounded in love, know the love of Christ that surpasses knowledge and be filled to all the fullness of God.

Prophetic Ways of Wisdom

Proverbs 14:35 says, "The king's favor is toward a servant who acts wisely." As we step out zealously in the gift of prophecy, let's pursue a heart of wisdom so we find favor with our King. After all, we are Jesus' servants as we share His testimony with the Body of Christ and with the world.

Michael Sullivant in *Prophetic Etiquette* has some masterful thoughts for us on the issue of gifts, fruit and wisdom. Let's ponder the words of one who has both moved in the prophetic and pastored prophetic people:

> There is a "prophetic etiquette" that needs to be taught and learned in the Lord's house so that the gift of prophecy can be utilized to its fullest intent and extent. Four governing values— love, integrity, humility and passionate pursuit. I have identified four basic values that will make prophecy more helpful if embraced. I am certain there are others that could be added to the list. Actually, these values do not apply only to prophecy, but also to any ministry in the body of Christ.[1]

With this in view, I have listed some valuable bullets of wisdom for your revelatory storehouse. They can help keep you from grieving the Holy Spirit and the hearts of those to whom you serve the word of the Lord.

- *Avoid prophesying your pet doctrine.* For pure stream to come forth, you must yield your favorite opinions and prejudices.
- *Refrain from scolding.* Do not lecture people through prophecy. Condemnation does not come from the Spirit of Christ (see Romans 8:1).
- *Avoid publicly correcting leadership through prophecy.* Honor those in authority. We are not called to criticize but to pray for them (see Romans 13:1–5; 1 Peter 2:17; Jude 8–9). Do not release words that create pressure for people to perform.
- *Be careful with your words.* Take care when speaking about courtship, marriages, births and deaths. Rare exceptions occur, but stick to the main and the plain. Do not put a heavy word on people, pressuring them into personal directions that violate their individual consciences.
- *Do not focus on problems.* Speaking only from known problems and current circumstances creates unnecessary stress. Prophesy life! See the problem but search out the solution. (I will share more about this in the reading for day 20.)
- *Avoid preaching.* Do not preach for extended periods under the guise of prophesying. Know when to stop. Do not use a gifting as a soapbox to display your latest revelation, but serve with humility to exalt Christ, not your own ego.
- *Refrain from redundant and repetitive prophecies.* When the mind of God has been clearly communicated by others, there is no need for another to jump in and say it over. Be encouraged knowing that you heard the Lord.
- *Stay in tune.* If prophesying during a meeting, stay in tune with the tenor of the meeting. Do not become a crosscurrent and frustrate the overall message of the Lord. A word wrongly spoken is like a clanging symbol. Outside of a meeting, perceive the context, the culture and God's heart

for that person or group. Always cultivate the culture of honor by respecting those in authority; otherwise, simply pray your word privately.

- *Speak inspirationally.* The ideal is to speak encouragingly and avoid yelling, whining or harshness. This is part of edifying and doing all things decently and in order.

- *Avoid confusion.* Refrain from speaking if you have an unclear or obscure message. If the trumpet makes an uncertain sound, it produces confusion (see 1 Corinthians 14:33). Simply push the pause button and continue to seek the Lord.

- *Stick to the Word.* This is especially true for beginners. Do not swim out too far from shore until you are sure your vessel is seaworthy. Be addicted to the Scriptures.

- *Refrain from injecting self.* Avoid inserting self and personal problems into your words. This includes moods, pressures, frustration, bitterness, haste, opinions, legalism or times when you are sick or on major medication. Be a clean vessel for the Lord to use.

- *Purge negative emotions.* It is important to let the Holy Spirit purge any negative elements from your spirit. Avoid speaking on issues on which you know you have negative emotional involvement. Be an intercessor in these situations, not a mouthpiece.

- *Stay within your measure of faith.* Step out, yet stay within your boundaries (see 2 Corinthians 10:15). "Since we have gifts that differ according to the grace given to us, each of us is to exercise them accordingly: if prophecy, according to the proportion of his faith" (Romans 12:6).

- *Be governed by love.* Let the love of Christ be your aim (see 1 Corinthians 13:1–3; 14:1; 2 Corinthians 5:14).

- *Do not subject yourself to the fear of people.* Shoot for the mark of the overall unity of the Body of Christ. Avoid the snare of the people-pleasing spirit and the fear of rejection. Strive for the goal of pleasing the Lord.

• *Remember: The major principle is edification.* Does this prophecy sound like Jesus? Will it build up this person, organization or church? Like weightlifters, let us learn to be Body-builders.

Lessons for the Beginner, Guidance for the Mature

Many mark 1988 as a year when the prophetic movement was reintroduced to the Body of Christ. This was one generation (or forty years) after the beginning of the Latter Rain movement and the birth of Israel as a nation. During the late '80s and early '90s I was privileged to be part of the company of prophetic voices emerging nationally. Here is some practical advice I wrote for getting started—lessons for beginners and a stake in the ground to which the mature can always return.[2]

1. *Earnestly desire the gifts of the Holy Spirit,* especially that you may prophesy (see 1 Corinthians 14:1). God wants to speak to you and through you.

2. *Trust the peace of God.* Beware speaking when your spirit is uneasy, in turmoil or feels forced to speak. Look for the peace of God in every word you hear (see Psalm 85:8; Philippians 4:7–9).

3. *Obey the urging of the Spirit.* Remember that the prophetic spirit is under your control. It will not impel you to speak against your better judgment. You can turn it off or turn it on by an act of your will.

4. *Do not rely on physical sensations.* When you begin to move in prophecy, the Lord frequently gives you physical sensations—knots in the stomach, fluttering heartbeats, intense heat, a feeling of euphoria, impressions, visions and so on. The Lord does this to prepare you to receive or deliver His word. As time goes on, however, the Lord

often withholds these promptings so you can grow in the ability to hear Him apart from physical sensations.

5. *Speak clearly and naturally.* You do not have to speak in King James English to get your point across. Nor do you always have to say, "Thus saith the Lord." If your word is truly from God, the Spirit will confirm it in the hearts of the listeners (see John 10:4–5, 16). Also, speak loudly and clearly enough to be heard by everyone.

6. *Timing is everything.* A prophecy that comes at the wrong time during a meeting sounds like a noisy gong or clanging symbol. It will draw attention to you, not to Jesus.

7. *Leave corrective and directional words to experienced and mature brothers and sisters.* The simple gift of prophecy is for exhortation, edification and comfort (see 1 Corinthians 14:3). If you do receive a directional word, write it down and submit it prayerfully to your leadership for evaluation.

8. *How do you receive a message?* You do not have to be struck by a lightning bolt to prophesy! A message can come in a variety of ways: literal words, dreams, senses or inklings, pictures of words like print in your mind and so on. More often than not, a seasoned prophet receives the sense of what God wants to say. Your duty is then to express that sense clearly and appropriately (see Psalm 12:6).

9. *What do you do with a word after you have received it?* That depends. Not all words are for the purpose of proclamation; many are for intercession. Some words should be put on file, waiting for confirmation. Others should be written down and submitted for evaluation by more mature Christians with a prophetic ministry. Some prophecies should be spoken only to an individual, others to a group. Some prophetic words are delivered as songs.

10. *What if you mess up?* No one is perfect. Maturity comes from taking risks and occasionally failing. Proverbs 24:16 says, "A righteous man falls seven times, and rises again." Learn from your mistakes, ask the Lord to forgive and cleanse you and get back up and humbly receive His grace (see 1 Peter 5:5).

Nine Scriptural Tests

The following nine Scripture tests on judging prophecy are inspired by teaching from Derek Prince.[3]

1. *Encouragement:* "One who prophesies speaks to men for edification and exhortation and consolation" (1 Corinthians 14:3). The end purpose of all true prophetic revelation is to build up, admonish and encourage the people of God. Anything not directed to this end is not true prophecy. Jeremiah's commission was negative at first, then given with a promise (see Jeremiah 1:5, 10). First Corinthians 14:12 sums it up best: "Seek to abound for the edification of the church."

2. *Agreement with Scripture:* "All Scripture is inspired by God" (2 Timothy 3:16). All true revelation agrees with the letter and spirit of Scripture. Read 2 Corinthians 1:17–20, where the Holy Spirit says *yea* and *amen* in Scripture. He also says *yea* and *amen* in revelation. He does not contradict Himself.

3. *Focused on Christ:* "He will glorify Me, for He will take of Mine and will disclose it to you" (John 16:14) All true revelation centers in Jesus Christ, and exalts and glorifies Him (Revelation 19:10).

4. *Fruit of the Holy Spirit:* "Beware of the false prophets, who come to you in sheep's clothing, but inwardly are ravenous wolves. You will know them by their fruits"

(Matthew 7:15–16). True revelation produces fruit in character and conduct that resembles the fruit of the Holy Spirit (see Galatians 5:22–23; Ephesians 5:9).

Among aspects of character or conduct produced that are clearly not the fruit of the Holy Spirit, we may mention the following: pride, arrogance, boastfulness, exaggeration, dishonesty, covetousness, financial irresponsibility, licentiousness, immorality, addictive appetites, broken marriage vows, broken homes. Any revelation responsible for results such as these is from a channel other than the Holy Spirit.

5. *Prophecy Fulfillment:* See Deuteronomy 18:20–22. If a revelation contains a prediction concerning the future that is not fulfilled, then (with a few exceptions) the revelation is not from God. Exceptions:

   a. When the will of the person is involved

   b. When it involves national repentance (e.g., Nineveh)

   c. When it concerns a Messianic prediction (hundreds of years until fulfilled)

6. *Obedience to God:* See Deuteronomy 13:1–5. The fact that a person makes a prediction concerning the future that is fulfilled does not necessarily prove he or she is moving by Holy Spirit–inspired revelation. If such a person, by his own ministry, turns others away from obedience to the one true God, then that person is false, even if he makes correct predictions concerning the future.

7. *Liberty:* "You have not received a spirit of slavery leading to fear again, but you have received a spirit of adoption as sons by which we cry out, 'Abba! Father!'" (Romans 8:15). True revelation given by the Holy Spirit produces liberty, not bondage (see 1 Corinthians 14:33; 2 Timothy 1:7). The Holy Spirit never brings God's people into a condition in which they act like slaves, motivated by fear or legal compulsion.

8. *Life:* "[God] made us adequate as servants of a new covenant, not of the letter but of the Spirit; for the letter kills, but the Spirit gives life" (2 Corinthians 3:6). True revelation given by the Holy Spirit produces life, not death.

9. *Inner Confirmation:* "As for you, the anointing which you received from Him abides in you, and you have no need for anyone to teach you; but as His anointing teaches you about all things, and is true and is not a lie, and just as it has taught you, you abide in Him" (1 John 2:27). True revelation given by the Holy Spirit is confirmed by the Spirit within the believer. The Holy Spirit is "the Spirit of Truth" (John 16:13). He bears witness to what is true and rejects what is false. This ninth test is the most subjective of them all, and must be used in conjunction with the previous eight objective standards.

Taking the Prophetic to the Streets

In past years the operation of our revelatory storehouse has been mostly in the setting of a typical congregational meeting. But, oh, there is so much more and some parts of the Body of Christ are finding great success as they prophesy outside the traditional four walls of the church building. Yes, the Church is to be built up *and* sent out.

Numbers 11 records what happened after God took off the Spirit that was upon Moses and placed Him upon the seventy elders. When the Spirit rested upon them, they all prophesied. At the same time, two other men, Eldad and Medad, also moved by the Holy Spirit, "prophesied in the camp" (verse 26). Some seemed to be offended at this, yet Moses refused to forbid these two men and there is no indication that they stopped. But after the seventy elders prophesied, "they did not do it again" (verse 25). They just used their gift at "church," went home and never did it again. How horrible! I trust and pray that you will explode for Jesus' sake and do some real damage to the kingdom of darkness outside the four walls of the church.

Consider the following and what stepping out in the prophetic might look like for you:

- Pursue a revelatory conversation with a waiter or waitress at a restaurant under the leadership of the Holy Spirit. (Sounds like Jesus counseling with the woman at the well to me.)
- Go to a New Age festival and wisely share the truth of God's Word. (Sounds like Paul going to Mars Hill.)
- Help an acquaintance with AIDS receive the Word of the Lord and get healed. (How about Elisha and his interaction with the leprous man in 2 Kings 5? Naaman's friends persuaded him to obey the word, and he got healed.)
- Go to a public park or bridge underpass to the homeless. Give them a meal and ask if you can pray for them. (Sounds like Jesus feeding the five thousand with a couple of buns and five fish.)

In addition to congregational settings, let's take the prophetic to the marketplace, the judicial system, the public school environment, the poor. Let's color outside the lines!

As you meditate and pray over the principles in this chapter, remember that the Holy Spirit is with you to teach and train you in the gift of prophecy. You will make some mistakes, but He will redeem every one of them if you humble yourself and receive His loving correction. Becoming God's faithful servant in the gift of prophecy will involve you in His intimate thoughts and plans for His children and for the lost souls of the world. Be encouraged as you step out in faith and dare to grow up in the testimony of the Lord Jesus Christ.

⟫ P R A Y E R ⟪

Father, I present myself to You right now and ask that You would grant me wisdom beyond my years to keep me on your straight and narrow path. Give me opportunity to impact the lives of others by allowing me to speak, pray and act out Your thoughts, O God—to edify, exhort and comfort others. Help me to pursue passionately, with great hunger, the spiritual gifts, especially that I might prophesy. I ask that my words would align with Your Word and bring life to those I encounter. Bring people across my path who need to hear from You, and grant me the boldness to speak on Your behalf and release Your love. Help me to serve revelation with wisdom to further Your Kingdom purposes. In Christ's name, Amen.

⮞ Embracing Your Calling—Day 10

1. What lessons in prophetic etiquette have you learned? Compare them to those in today's reading.

2. What are some of the scriptural guidelines or tests for judging prophecy?

3. Think of a key prophecy you have received. Which scriptural tests show you that it was an accurate word from God?

4. Ask God for an opportunity to step out in the prophetic outside the church building—in your neighborhood, at work, with a friend. Pause right now and ask the Lord to bring someone to mind that He wants to encourage through you. Ask Him, "God, what are Your thoughts for this person?" Listen and share those thoughts with that person this week.

The Anatomy of a Prophetic Word

*Counsel in the heart of man is like water in a deep
well, but a man of understanding will draw it out.*

PROVERBS 20:5, AMP

To release the revelatory counsel of God correctly, we need *His understanding.* There are at least ten principles concerning revelatory gifts that we must understand so that we will not dismiss a genuine word of God or diminish the impact He wants that word to produce.

I have had the privilege of walking and conversing with many of God's choice servants. Much of what follows is what I have gleaned over many years from these divergent voices. I have held on to these precious truths and added my own insights along the way. As we look at these factors, we will gain a better understanding of the anatomy of a prophetic word and how it works to bring about the results God desires. Let's get the most out of each word that we can.

1. The Source of Revelation

There are three possible sources of revelation.

Source #1: God

"Beloved, do not believe every spirit, but test the spirits to see whether they are from God, because many false prophets have gone out into the world" (1 John 4:1). There can be mixture in a revelatory word—not because the word is mixed when it comes from God but because it is filtered through the tainted soul of a man or woman. It can be flavored with our unsanctified opinions, prejudices and emotions. This is particularly true in the area of our learning to interpret and apply the prophetic word.

Source #2: Self

"I did not send these prophets, but they ran. I did not speak to them, but they prophesied" (Jeremiah 23:21; see also Ezekiel 13:1–2). These prophets spoke out of the inspiration of their own souls or hearts. They were prophesying what they wanted instead of what God was really saying at the time. This is why we must emphasize the centrality of the cross of Jesus—because we must die to our own desires.

Source #3: Satan

"[Jesus] turned and said to Peter, 'Get behind Me, Satan! You are a stumbling block to Me; for you are not setting your mind on God's interests, but man's'" (Matthew 16:23). Peter had just spoken by the gift of prophecy when he declared, "You are the Christ, the Son of the living God" (verse 16). Then, as Jesus referred prophetically to His own crucifixion, Peter protested and elicited this strong rebuke. One minute Peter was speaking by inspiration of the prophetic, and the next he was disagreeing with Jesus, whose words did not line up with his own strong-willed opinion. Peter thus became an instrument of Satan to speak in opposition to the purposes of God.

Our own preconceived, prejudicial mind-sets can hinder us from rightly interpreting or responding to revelation. The enemy uses these mindsets to twist and diminish true revelation from God, as well as to fabricate his own supposed revelations that oppose the purposes of God.

Looking to God

We must recognize that revelation comes from one of these three major sources. Yet as believers in Christ we must also accept that if we ask our Father, in Jesus' name, He will give us good gifts. Let's trust the Holy Spirit.

2. Modes of Revelation

God has limitless ways to communicate with His followers. The greatest mode of revelation, however, comes from two sources: the written Word and the living Word.

The following scriptural examples portray the diversity of tools the Holy Spirit uses to release the voice of God to people:

- The powerful, majestic voice of the Lord in water, in thunder, in breaking cedar trees, flames of fire, shaking the wilderness and stripping the forest bare (see Psalm 29)
- God speaking once, twice, through a dream, vision (see Job 33:14–18)
- A voice in a trance (see Acts 10:9–16)
- The voice of many angels (see Revelation 5:11)
- The voice of the archangel (see 1 Thessalonians 4:16)
- The sound of many waters (see Revelation 1:15)

- The sound of the Lord walking in the Garden (see Genesis 3:8)
- The sound of the army of God marching in the tops of the trees (see 2 Samuel 5:23–25)
- The audible voice of God (see Exodus 3:4)
- God speaking peace to His people (see Psalm 85:8)
- God's written Word as our primary source of His voice (see Psalm 119:105)
- Wonders in the sky and on the earth (see Joel 2:30–31)
- Visions and parables given to the prophets (see Hosea 12:10)
- Words and physical metaphors given to the prophets (see Jeremiah 18:1–6)
- The Holy Spirit speaking to a group (see Acts 13:2)
- Men moved by the Holy Spirit declaring God's voice (see 2 Peter 1:21)
- Heavenly visitation in which one is brought up before the Lord (see 2 Corinthians 12:1–4)
- The Holy Spirit bearing witness to our spirits (see Romans 8:16)
- A donkey speaking with the voice of a man (see 2 Peter 2:16)
- One person speaking the revelatory counsel of the Lord to another (see James 5:19–20)
- In these last days, God's own Son (see Hebrews 1:2)

3. Proper Interpretation

Numerous genuine words have been judged false because of wrong interpretation. The opposite can be true as well. False words can be deemed appropriate due to a lack of discernment and inadequate interpretation skills. We must seek the Lord, therefore, for wise counsel and wise counselors.

Special examples in Scripture show us the need for wedding prophetic revelation with accurate interpretation. Through the process of seeking God for understanding, we build faith in God's desire to communicate with us, and confidence in our own ability to hear His voice. Like Joseph, we can also declare, "Do not interpretations belong to God?" (Genesis 40:8).

Recall the account of Peter's vision (revelation) when the Lord declared all animals clean in His sight. This did not sit well with Peter's good Jewish upbringing, which dictated that certain animals were unclean and should not be eaten. When Peter awoke and pondered the Lord's declaration, he "wondered within himself what this vision which he had seen meant" (Acts 10:17, NKJV). Peter needed understanding to benefit from the vision.

In Acts 11 Peter had gained the proper interpretation of the vision, as he was now speaking with brothers astonished that he had eaten with "uncircumcised men" (verse 3). This was a turnaround that affected all of Church history.

4. Determining the Best Application

The apostle Paul provides us with a fascinating, poignant example of how important proper application of properly interpreted revelation really is. He had been hearing in every city, through the Holy Spirit, that "bonds and afflictions await me" in Jerusalem (Acts 20:23). The prophet Agabus actually "took Paul's belt and bound his own feet and hands, and said, 'This is what the Holy Spirit says: "In this way the Jews at Jerusalem will bind the man who owns this belt and deliver him into the hands of the Gentiles"'" (Acts 21:11). Paul's friends "began begging him not to go up to Jerusalem" (verse 12).

Would the apostle not be better off avoiding certain death and prolonging his ministry to the churches? But Paul knew the

Lord was leading him to Jerusalem and giving him opportunity to count the cost. He was ready, he said, "not only to be bound, but even to die at Jerusalem for the name of the Lord Jesus" (verse 13).

Paul did not let the affection or emotional display of those who loved him persuade him to stop. What an incredible example of the discernment and tenacity of a totally committed soul! *Lord, build in us this wisdom and surround us with people who will accept Your will for our lives and support us as we step out in faith.*

5. Appropriation: Calling It Forth

"This command I entrust to you, Timothy, my son, in accordance with the prophecies previously made concerning you, that by them you fight the good fight" (1 Timothy 1:18). When a prophetic word comes to us, what do we do with it? We have been taught to hold it with an open hand before God and trust Him to bring it to pass. This is, I believe, a true teaching. But we must also respond to the word with faith and obedience.

6. Searching for the Conditional Clauses

Often there are conditions behind words of prophecy that must be met in order for the word to be fulfilled. *Sometimes these conditions are present in the heart of God but not spoken to the minds of people.* This is a principle we do not like, because all we really want to do is get a word from God and then go on our merry way. Our flesh does not want to press in to the heart of the Father to find out if some requirement or qualification might be involved.

But God's words are designed to draw us to Him in relationship. He desires to communicate with us intimately about His plans for our lives, so He makes it necessary for us to seek Him for more understanding about His words. If *we* will, *He* will! Most words do not automatically come into being. We must seek the Lord for the conditional clauses that must be met.

Here are some conditions set forth in scriptural words from God.

- Turning from evil (see Jeremiah 18:8)
- Humility, prayer and repentance (see 2 Chronicles 7:14)
- Looking to God for mercy (see 2 Kings 20:1–5; Jonah 3:4, 10)

7. The Kairos Moment: The Timing of a Matter

Being able to discern the timing of a word of prophecy is sometimes crucial to the proper impact of the revelation. It takes practice, patience and wisdom to discern timing accurately, but the Lord gives us great grace and is very patient with us as we learn. The Greek word *kairos* refers to an appointed and strategic time for a matter to come into being. The Lord may give us revelation far in advance of the actual manifestation in the natural realm. He may require us to hold it in our hearts until a strategic time, when the word can be received with grace by those who are to receive it.

This has been the case in my ministry experience. In 1979 I had a brief encounter with a young Korean man. A snapshot picture went off inside me, and I knew he had a calling of apostolic proportions with a power gift to release in the nations. But I prayed and wept over that word for fifteen years before I had the release and *kairos* divine appointment to do anything with it. Today this man, Dr. Ché Ahn, heads up a wonderful, fast-growing network of churches called Harvest International Ministries across the world.

Timing is everything! Learning to discern the timing of the Lord becomes a great test of character in our lives. As we wait on Him for direction and fulfillment of revelation, God is patiently weaving His character into the tapestry of our lives.

8. Proper Heart Motivation

God looks deeply into the heart of a man or woman to find his or her inner motivation. Do we want glory for the Lord or promotion before people? He is a loving but jealous God, and out of His mercy He searches the hearts of His people for idols that would take His place. Paul writes, "The love of Christ constrains us, because we judge thus: that if One died for all, then all died; and He died for all, that those who live should live no longer for themselves, but for Him who died for them and rose again" (2 Corinthians 5:14–15, NKJV). Love for God, and not the love of recognition or approval from people, should be our motivation.

9. Surface-Level Contradictions

On some occasions the Holy Spirit speaks very clearly, but when the promise is being birthed, it can appear quite different from what we expected it to look like. We have to cry out to the Lord so we will not miss the day of our visitation, due to misunderstanding the manner in which the promise first appeared.

Three ways to deal with surface-level contradictions include the following:

Acknowledge Deeper Principles

"Unto us a Child is born, unto us a Son is given" (Isaiah 9:6, NKJV). Israel was looking for the birth of a king. She expected a child of royal birth; instead she got a little boy born in a stable to poor parents. This was beyond her comprehension. God was employing principles of pride and humility that she could not understand. The circumstances of Jesus' birth seemed to contradict the promise the Lord had given.

Trust God with the Contradictions

When Joseph first learned that Mary, his fiancée, was pregnant, he decided to put her away secretly because, to his mind, it seemed like the righteous thing to do (Matthew 1:18–19). It came out of his own heart of compassion and his principled thinking. He could have been saying to himself, *Let's just ignore this prophetic revelation about a virgin being pregnant (who happens to be my betrothed!) and just hide it away.*

But something happened to Joseph as he was contemplating these things. He had a second revelation that changed him (verses 20–21). God visited him with revelation to dispel the fear and bring him faith to believe in the prophetic word already spoken. "And Joseph awoke from his sleep and did as the angel of the Lord commanded him, and took Mary as his wife" (verse 24).

When things appear contradictory, we must learn to trust Him—trust Him with our whole heart!

Discern the Paradox

"Elijah said to Ahab, 'Go up, eat and drink; for there is the sound of the roar of a heavy shower'" (1 Kings 18:41). In this passage Elijah was proclaiming something that was not happening. It had not rained for three and a half years; it was dry as dust. Yet this guy was proclaiming, "I hear rain, and it's a deluge."

Definitely sounds like a contradiction to me! Then Elijah sent out his servant to look. He came back and said nothing was happening. Seven times he did this, until finally that little cloud that was only the size of a man's hand appeared. Even that report seems like a contradiction, because Elijah heard a roar, and this little cloud could not produce such a downpour. But eventually the sky grew black and the deluge came.

We must learn to discern things that appear paradoxical and not despise the day of small beginnings.

10. Properly Discerning the Ways of God and Humankind

I saved one of the best points for last. I think I will hear a sigh of relief from the prophetic company and a shout of *Amen!* from the recipients of their words.

One of the greatest potential problems for prophetic persons is that others assume they are in the gift mode whenever they speak. This not only shows lack of wisdom on the part of listeners; it also dishonors the prophetic persons. We must prayerfully, with godly, trusted counsel, seek proper discernment.

Speaking from One's Natural Mind

Consider this example. Until God corrected him, Nathan spoke to David out of his natural mind:

> The king said to Nathan the prophet, "See now, I dwell in a house of cedar, but the ark of God dwells within tent curtains." Nathan said to the king, "Go, do all that is in your mind, for the LORD is with you." But in the same night the word of the LORD came to Nathan, saying, "Go and say to My servant David, 'Thus says the LORD, "Are you the one who should build Me a house to dwell in?"'"
>
> 2 Samuel 7:2–5

David could have taken that initial directive as a prophetic word to proceed with his plans, and it would not have been the revelation of God. (As God planned it, David did not end up building the Temple, but rather his son Solomon.)

Prophets Are Just People

When Samuel was sent to the house of Jesse to anoint one of his sons as king, the prophet had no idea which one he would anoint. God's word of instruction contained no information as to which son it would be. As Samuel looked at the firstborn son of Jesse, he thought (in part out of his good Jewish tradition) that Eliab would be the one, because he looked good and the firstborn usually got the birthright. But no. As the divine checkmark of God went across his heart, he had to stop, listen and get discernment quickly!

This example from 1 Samuel 16 contains important principles about proper discernment. Just because someone has a mature gifting does not mean all his or her thoughts and statements are genuine words from the Lord. Do not make the mistake of assuming that every word that comes out of his or her mouth in natural conversation is some sort of high-level word. We need to allow people with prophetic graces to function as normally as anyone else. They are just people!

Years ago when my children were younger, people would approach my wife and me when we had our children with us—in a mall or at church—looking for a prophetic word. I knew they were hungry for God. But my kids were hungry to have a dad! I just had to say, "Sorry, I'm being a dad right now, not a prophet." Some people turned away at times disgusted. But I had other priorities in life; I am not a jukebox on which someone can push the buttons anytime to play a tune. We must learn when to "step into the gift" and when to "step out."

We must not take ourselves too seriously, either, if the revelatory gifting flows from time to time in our own lives. We all have room to grow, and we need to make allowances for others.

Our Goal Is Christ and Christ Glorified

The ultimate goal of the prophetic is to reveal Christ. So the lifestyle of a prophet or those who walk in the prophetic should pull back the veil that the god of this age has put on the minds of unbelievers so they cannot see the light of the Gospel of the glory of Jesus Christ (see 2 Corinthians 4:3–4). When these wisdom parameters are in place, they will create a safe atmosphere where we can walk into fruitful prophetic maturation and faith can move freely.

⟩ P R A Y E R ⟨

Father, thank You for the privilege of being a voice for You. Help me to discern Your voice as my sole source of revelation. Open new modes of revelation so that I can see and know You more. I ask for Your divine wisdom to make proper interpretation and application and the proper timing for its release. Give me grace to wait on You with patience as You weave Your own character and wisdom into my life. I trust You and thank You for choosing to use weak vessels to display Your glory. I am one of those vessels, and I bless other prophetic vessels You have chosen to speak Your word. Let Your word go forth and accomplish all that it was set out to do. In Jesus' great name, Amen.

▓ Embracing Your Calling—Day 11

1. At times what seems to be a contradiction can be an accurate fulfillment of the revelation. Give an account of this from Scripture and also from your personal experience if possible.

2. Give an account from your own life when you misinterpreted a prophetic word. What was the result?

3. How have you responded to prophetic words in the past with faith and obedience? What has been the result?

4. Examine the tenderness of the soil of your heart. Are there rocks in your heart? Ask the Holy Spirit to reveal any hard places, then call for His tenderizing agent to be released.

The Peaks of a Prophetic Lifestyle

What makes a roller coaster exhilarating? Is it not the extremes created by climbing to the highest peak in the park and then plunging downward at top speed? Without the highs and lows of the ride, it just would not be a ride.

Living a prophetic lifestyle is similar in that it has some incredible peaks coupled with deep (and sometimes dark) valleys. The ride is not always pleasant, but it is definitely always an adventure and ultimately satisfying if we make the most out of every situation.

Before we look at some of these peaks and valleys in the next two day's readings, first we must identify the two foundational purposes for the prophetic. Without a clear understanding of these two foundational purposes, we will misuse revelation and miss the main objectives of living a prophetic lifestyle.

Purpose #1: Testifying about Jesus

As followers of Jesus, we are to carry the fire of the testimony of Christ—a longing to know Him and to make Him known.

Glimpsing details of the future or making glorious statements cannot be our primary motivation. *The enflaming passion for knowing this glorious Man, Christ Jesus, and for making Him known, is the empowering force within that will cause us to exude the fragrance of His wonderful presence.* Without this solid foundation in place, we will expend our energy for no eternal purpose and fail to reveal the testimony of Jesus through our lives.

> He was asking His disciples, "Who do people say that the Son of Man is?" And they said, "Some say John the Baptist; and others, Elijah; but still others, Jeremiah, or one of the prophets." He said to them, "But who do you say that I am?" Simon Peter answered, "You are the Christ, the Son of the living God." And Jesus said to him, "Blessed are you, Simon Barjona, because flesh and blood did not reveal this to you, but My Father who is in heaven."
>
> Matthew 16:13–17

There was much debate over who Jesus really was and what He was about. Many looked at His marvelous works and mannerisms and compared Him to prophets who had come before Him. These observers used their natural understanding to explain who He was. But Peter received his understanding from the Father, God Himself.

True prophetic revelation comes from no other source but the living God. We cannot figure Him out by natural perception or educated guesses. Peter received a personal testimony of Jesus from the Spirit of God, then spoke it out by the power of the spirit of prophecy. Once Peter (along with the other disciples) had received the testimony of Jesus, then the Father revealed to Peter who Jesus was: "I also say to you that you are Peter, and upon this rock I will build My church; and the gates of Hades will not overpower it" (Matthew 16:18).

Jesus was saying to Peter (*petra*—a little stone) that the Church would be built on the large Rock, Jesus, and that hell itself could not prevail against it. That solid foundation is the revelation of Jesus Christ, and no storm can blow you off that Rock.

It takes the Holy Spirit to know who God is—to show us who Jesus is. The Holy Spirit is the first Person of the Godhead we meet. He takes Jesus from being some religious icon and illuminates Him as the Christ, the Son of God. He makes Jesus real to us.

The Holy Spirit also releases the spirit of conviction of sin, righteousness and judgment to come on our lives, and thereby reveals the centrality, the glories and the wonders of this glorious Man, Christ Jesus. As the saying goes, *It takes God to know God!* This is the foundation of the prophetic. If prophetic revelation does not make us fall more in love with Jesus, then we have missed its main purpose.

The true purpose of the prophetic is not only to reveal the Man Jesus but also to reveal the Lordship of Jesus. "No one can say, 'Jesus is Lord,' except by the Holy Spirit" (1 Corinthians 12:3). We cannot understand Jesus' Lordship and His right to authority over our lives without the revelation of the Holy Spirit operating in our behalf.

The revelation of Christ Jesus and His Lordship is the foundational purpose and focus of all prophetic revelation. If we are not fully grounded here, we will have no prophetic revolution.

Purpose #2: To Pierce Defenses

The Holy Spirit is the master at detecting and piercing the defenses of the enemy, and He uses prophetic "gracelets" as antitank missiles. Jesus demonstrated this second purpose of the prophetic in His interaction with Nathanael in John 1:45–51 and with the woman at the well in John 4:7–26. Jesus' execution of prophetic revelation pierced their defenses of skepticism and prejudice and cut through to the hidden places in their hearts. The Holy Spirit anointed Jesus to reveal these hidden things in order to bring these individuals to the understanding that He was the Messiah.

Piercing the Defense of Skepticism

Nathanael had just been approached by Philip, who had told him that they had found the One "of whom Moses in the Law and also the Prophets wrote—Jesus of Nazareth, the son of Joseph" (John 1:45).

> Nathanael said to him, "Can any good thing come out of Nazareth?" Philip said to him, "Come and see." Jesus saw Nathanael coming to Him, and said of him, "Behold, an Israelite indeed, in whom there is no deceit!" Nathanael said to Him, "How do You know me?" Jesus answered and said to him, "Before Philip called you, when you were under the fig tree, I saw you." Nathanael answered Him, "Rabbi, You are the Son of God; You are the King of Israel."
>
> verses 46–49

Even though Nathanael appeared skeptical in his response to Philip about Jesus as the promised Messiah, the Lord saw by the spirit of revelation that he was being true to his understanding. Nathanael was speaking honestly and transparently, calling a spade a spade. But Nathanael was shocked that Jesus professed to know him even though they had never laid eyes on one another. Jesus' word of knowledge about the fig tree served only to confirm to Nathanael that this was no ordinary man. Jesus' revelation of God's pure view of Nathanael's heart pierced his defense of skepticism.

Piercing the Defense of Sin

In a second prophetic account we see a stark contrast between Jesus and the woman at the well. Because He was a Jew, there was an immediate barrier between Him and this woman. Hebrews had nothing to do with the half-breed Samaritans. A good Jew considered them less than nothing. Not only that, but she was an adulterous woman who worshiped false gods, and He was a pure single man. They could not have been any more separate than if a brick wall had stood between them.

Yet Jesus, by the power of the spirit of prophecy, dared to break through the wall of tradition and prejudice and reach out to a lost soul. She was touched not only by His daring to speak with her, but by the fact that He knew what her personal life was like.

> He said to her, "Go, call your husband and come here." The woman answered and said, "I have no husband." Jesus said to her, "You have correctly said, 'I have no husband'; for you have had five husbands, and the one whom you now have is not your husband; this you have said truly."
>
> John 4:16–18

Jesus' penetrating revelation had the power to break down her defenses and convince her that He was a prophet—better yet, the Messiah! Soon she ran out and told the whole town about the man who must be the Christ, "a man who told me all the things that I have done" (verse 29). God had exposed the deceitfulness of her life, and she knew that God knew her. Awesome! Not only did she experience a swift change in her personal history, but she turned her city upside down. Personal transformation can lead to a city transformation, if you let it.

An Airport Encounter

Years ago I was coming back from a crusade on the island nation of Haiti with my dear friend Mahesh Chavda, and we had a layover in Atlanta. The meetings had been wonderful and we had seen many miracles, such as a 77-year-old woman, blind from birth, being given her sight on the last night we were there. As some of us from the team, including my sister, were sitting in the airport in the afterglow of success, an unkempt man appeared. His hair was a mess, his clothes were ragged and he reeked of nicotine from his chain-smoking. On top of all that, he was wearing one of those sandwich board signs with something like *Prophets Are of No Profit* written on it.

As he approached, I became agitated, feeling protective of my sister and wary of his coming too close. Then he flopped down in the same row of chairs we were occupying, just a few seats away.

As we were contemplating moving, suddenly my spiritual antennae went up and I began to ask the Lord if He had something to say about this man. As I prayed quietly in the Spirit, the Lord began to speak to me about the man. Then, in question form, I began to address him.

"Sir, you've been really wounded by the Body of Christ, haven't you?"

The man turned his head and looked at me.

"In fact," I continued, "you've been kicked out of the church you'd been part of. Is that right?"

He continued to stare.

"And you don't have a place to live. You've been living out of a garage. Is that right?"

Tears began coming down his face.

"And your wife left you about three years ago, and you've been rejected by the Body of Christ, and you carry great pain in your life."

As soon as I started speaking out of the place of compassion, the lens of judgment came off and I knew the Lord was speaking to the man's heart. By then a lot of tears were dripping onto the floor, as the people with me on the team were weeping, too, and repenting for their own judgmental attitudes.

The man responded by saying all of this was true. Then we stood to our feet and embraced one another. I prayed for the Lord's cleansing to come into his life and for healing to come into his heart.

I tell you the truth, the spirit of prophecy breaks down barriers and defenses. Even more than that, the Holy Spirit—the prophetic presence of God—can build bridges with people who are totally unlike us.

Revelatory gifting is part of God's defense system that releases missiles and destroys the defenses and barriers erected by the enemy to cut off the plan of God. What power we wield through the prophetic! If we want to use these powerful missiles with greater accuracy and effectiveness, we must deploy them with love and the testimony of our Lord Jesus Christ resounding in our hearts.

Now, remembering these two foundational purposes, let's move on to look at five peaks of a prophetic lifestyle and ministry.

Peak #1: When It Really Works!

In January 1994 I went to a city in Albania on the northern coast of the Adriatic Sea.

Albania is an Islamic nation that came under the control of Communism, and was opened in 1990 and 1991. In 1967 all church buildings were destroyed. Most of the people were also closed to the Gospel. In the Albanian language the name of the city we were visiting, Sein Gein, means St. John. Residents claim it is a city where the apostle John ministered. The evangelistic team I was with knew of only five or six Christians in the whole town.

Before we were scheduled to begin the evangelistic meeting— one of the first this town had seen maybe even in centuries—I was standing on a cliff overlooking the Adriatic Sea. I began asking the Lord, "What do You have for the people of Sein Gein?" Although we were there for only one night, I could sense their destiny with God, knowing that possibly John, the apostle, had walked that very spot.

Suddenly the name *Sarah* floated through my mind.

Again I said, "But Lord, what do You have for these people of Albania?"

Again the name *Sarah* ran through my mind.

Then it was time for the meeting. "Oh, well," I said, and made my way back down the bluff.

Only a few in the small gathering of eighty to a hundred people were Christians. A friend of mine shared his testimony. Then it was time for me to preach.

About halfway through my talk on Jesus Christ—the same yesterday, today and forever—that name *Sarah* floated through my mind again. So I turned to my interpreter and asked how to say *Sarah* in Albanian.

"Sabrina," he said.

So through the interpreter I asked if someone was present named Sabrina. Almost at the back of the building, a young woman raised her hand. I called her to come up front.

As Sabrina stood in front of the interpreter, the thought came to me to tell her how old she was. (Strange thought to tell a woman!) Then I asked the interpreter to tell her the following things: "Your name is Sabrina. You have never been to a Christian meeting before in your life. You are 32 years old. You have a tumor in your left breast. And Jesus wants to heal you."

As the Holy Spirit moved on Sabrina, a Muslim, it looked as though the rest of the people present had their eyeballs popping out! Sabrina got saved right on the spot.

After that wonderful meeting, it was raining. The other team members and I grabbed the first available car and driver. As this gentleman was driving us to the next town to spend the night, I suddenly got the feeling that I was like Philip, who climbed into the chariot with the Ethiopian eunuch in Acts 8.

"Jesus knows your name," I said to this driver through my interpreter. "He knows how many hairs are on your head. In fact, a woman at the meeting tonight, Sabrina, is thirty-two years old and had a tumor in her left breast. She's a Muslim, has never been to a Christian meeting before. But tonight she met the Lord Jesus Christ!"

As we headed down the bumpy old road, the driver started shaking. Guess what? Sabrina was his wife! I led him to the Lord as he drove the car that rainy night.

That kind of peak in the prophetic ministry ruins you, for sure! I want to see hundreds of thousands more of these demonstrations of God's revelatory power and love.

Peak #2: When Character Matches Prophetic Giftedness

In Section 1 on "The Lifestyle of Intimacy," I stressed the importance of maintaining "character to carry the gift." When our character and fruit match the gifting God graces us with, it seems as though He drops an extra portion of anointing on us called "the authority of God." We do not have to say or do anything different from before, but God puts a little extra seal of His life on us. When He puts His authority on our words, people stop to listen. What a peak!—and a new test as well.

Peak #3: When the Prophetic Spirit Is Imparted to Others

It is a peak and a privilege to impart God's presence to others. One of my chief joys is giving the measure of prophetic presence that I have to others. What a joy to equip others and teach them how to drink in the prophetic presence of Jesus in their lives! But true transformation of our culture will come about only as we each walk as carriers of His presence.

Peak #4: When We Embrace the Cross and Are Changed

A prophetic lifestyle is not easy. Going through dark valleys feels horrible emotionally. It can cause torment and bruising. But I can truthfully say that I would not trade those times of learning for anything. Do not let the devil keep you in a dark place; go to the cross and be transformed.

Making mistakes is also hard, especially when dealing with people. Learn all you can, even when you make mistakes. Keep going. Be like Paul, the apostle, who said, "Brethren, I do not regard myself as having laid hold of it yet; but one thing I do: forgetting what lies behind and reaching forward to what lies ahead, I press on toward the goal for the prize of the upward call of God in Christ Jesus" (Philippians 3:13–14).

Embracing the cross in the midst of life's difficulties and when we make mistakes is good and needful. It, too, is a peak in your prophetic life and ministry.

Peak #5: When We Step Aside and Jesus Is Glorified

The highest peak of a prophetic lifestyle is this: *Jesus Christ magnified, Jesus Christ glorified, Jesus Christ lifted up, and the life of God being released to other people.* This happens when a man or woman follows the two foundational purposes of prophetic ministry—knowing Christ and making Him known to others, and using prophetic words as missiles to pierce the defenses of the enemy. Once we get past the cross, resurrection life awaits us on the other side. It is then that we have stepped out of the way, and only Jesus can be seen. When He alone is magnified, we have reached the real peak of success.

⟩ P R A Y E R ⟨

Gracious heavenly Father, I am amazed at the awesome power You have displayed in all creation. I worship You for the tender grace and mercy You display through the testimony of Your Son, Jesus Christ. Thank You for the unimaginable sacrifice You made so that I can have life— life to the full. I am grateful for the victory I can walk in because of Your amazing love and grace to me. Lord, my desire is to be a carrier of the glorious presence of the Man, Christ Jesus. Work in me so that my character can hold Your glory and carry the gifts You have entrusted to me. I embrace You and Your work in my life. My desire is to glorify You, magnify You on this earth and loyally serve You in the fields of harvest. For the glory of Jesus, Amen.

⫸ Embracing Your Calling—Day 12

1. What are the two foundational purposes of the prophetic?

2. How have you seen these purposes manifest in your life?

3. What are some of the peaks you have experienced in prophetic ministry? How have they glorified Jesus?

4. Pause and thank God for the peaks you have been able to experience. Consider how Jesus has been magnified, and commit afresh to making Him known to others as you live a prophetic lifestyle in this world.

The Valleys of a
Prophetic Lifestyle

In the same way that there are glorious peaks of a prophetic lifestyle and ministry, there are numerous valleys that you may encounter. Snares and hostility await us as we venture forward. Some of them can feel like what David called "the valley of the shadow of death" (Psalm 23:4). Just know that in these valleys we are to "fear no evil" because He is with us. Let's now look at six of these valleys.

Valley #1: Hostility

The risk is not so much in wrongly promoting the prophetic as it is in putting prophets to death with the sword of the tongue. All throughout biblical and Church history and into the present time, there have been many misconceptions about prophets and prophecy that lead to hostility toward prophetic people. "The prophet is a fool, the inspired man is demented" (Hosea 9:7). What are some of the reasons for such hostility? Here are four.

Human Sin

The original sin of humankind is rebellion against God's word. Our hearts harbor hostility toward the entrance of God's word. The Holy Spirit does an intrusive work that brings the cutting edge of conviction, making us feel discomfort or outright pain. It is natural to resist these feelings. Prophetic revelation is a sharp knife! But remember, the revelatory word does not compete with the Word of God (Scripture); it complements it. And because of the sin in the human heart, hostility often arises not only toward God's Word but toward prophetic revelation.

The "Offensive" Way Gifts are Packaged

"God has chosen the foolish things of the world to shame the wise" (1 Corinthians 1:27). He often packages His gifts in an offensive manner. Moses is an excellent example of offensive packaging. He grew up with a silver spoon in his mouth, as an Egyptian prince in Pharaoh's house. He offended the Israelites ethnically, racially and socially. But God chose him as their deliverer. That does not compute in the religiously correct mind!

Paul is another example of offensive packaging. "On the contrary, seeing that I had been entrusted with the gospel to the uncircumcised . . ." (Galatians 2:7). Paul was a blueblood Pharisee sent to bring the message of salvation to the Gentiles, who despised the Jews because of their attitude of separation and religious superiority. Go figure! As some say today, "God offends the mind to reveal the heart."

The Veiled Way God Chooses to Reveal Himself

God's methodology also arouses hostility and creates snares. Numbers 12:6 addresses His methodology:

[The Lord] said, "Hear now My words: If there is a prophet among you, I, the LORD, shall make Myself known to him in a vision. I shall speak with him in a dream. Not so, with My servant Moses, he is faithful in all My household; with him I speak mouth to mouth, even openly, and not in dark sayings."

God has chosen to speak prophetically in various veiled ways. How did Jesus do most of His teaching? Through parables. Why would God purposely choose to create obscure messages? To create in us seeking hearts and the grace of humility, and because He is more than an answer box. He provokes questions within us to whet our appetites and stir up divine curiosity so we will seek the answer—God Himself! His desire is to draw us into closer communion and relationship through our seeking.

Lack of Appreciation for the Prophetic Process

Most people do not appreciate what many teach as a three-stage process: revelation, interpretation, application. After *revelation* comes, we must get proper *interpretation*; but proper *application* of the interpretation is also vitally important. Many receive the revelation initially but forget to finish the process by interpreting and applying it. Then they become hostile toward the messenger because they view it all as so complicated. Our tendency is to want revelation, interpretation and application dropped into our laps without our having to consult personally with the Source of revelation, the Holy Spirit. Remember that prophecy is designed to promote relationship. Hence, hostility arises out of a lack of true appreciation for the process of receiving God's word through relationship.

Valley #2: The Effects of Hostility on the Prophet

Gifted creatures often react in unhealthy ways to the hostility directed at them. After all, if you are getting stoned, it is natural to want to run and hide, or to build up a wall to avoid the wounding of those stones! But such natural reactions ensnare and paralyze prophetic people. As a result, they become:

Adversarial. Prophetic people may begin to look at the people who have reacted with hostility toward their revelations as the enemy, instead of recognizing that our real enemy, the devil, is the one stirring up reactions. Sin is our enemy, not sinners.

Judgmental. The pain of experiencing hostility can cause prophetic people to judge the motivation of everyone who disagrees with them. Then, in turn, they become overly critical of others.

Isolated. As the pain continues to fester, prophetic persons may isolate themselves and refuse to submit to any counsel, correction or authority within the local church. They are now lone rangers taking potshots at their brothers and sisters for whom Jesus died.

Dropouts. Finally prophetic people under attack may choose to drop out of the ranks of the local church and give up on the Body of Christ. Isolation leads to alienation. Alienation creates quitters.

Valley #3: Confusion over Personal Identity

Prophetic people often seem to be extra-sensitive. That is partially the means by which we get revelation. We are receptive to the gentle nudging of the Spirit. This sensitivity can enable us to perceive things quickly in the spirit realm. God created us this way. But if our personal identity and security rest on the wrong things, that sensitivity can cause us to overreact to certain words, innuendoes, judgments or criticisms from others.

Gaining a deep understanding of the following points can help us avoid those personal identity valleys.

Personal Identity Valleys

Your identity is who you are, not what you do. Your primary identity is found in who you are in Christ, not what you do in obedience to Him. You are a child of God and your identity is found in your relationship with Him. I love prophetic ministry. It is exhilarating and exciting. But I am first a child of God, not a prophetic minister. I have many roles in the earth—father, teacher, minister, intercessor—but none of these roles makes me who I am. They only tell you what I do in response to being a child of God created in His image. Do not build your foundation of identity on what you do, either in the ministry or in earthly responsibilities, or you will be blown away with the changing of the winds.

Your function is what you do. The same is true for gifts ministry. The ministry gifts with which God graces us are not who we are. These gifts enable us to function as dispensers of the love and mercy of our Creator. But our function will go through many changes. Who we are in Christ remains constant. Thank God!

You are not what you do. We are to be identified as true and authentic Christians who bear the resemblance of our Father God and carry the family name. Paul, an apostle, never identified himself as such, but called himself "a bond-slave of the Lord Jesus Christ." Also, if we label ourselves "Apostle Jones" or "Prophet Smith" and it is not true, we diminish the identity and function of that position in the Body of Christ. If I am to be called anything, it will not be because I put it on a business card or fancy website. It will be because fruit has been borne and others have eaten of it. Again, functions change. We are Christians first. Others are to declare who we are by the fruit borne. May a revolution occur even in this simple arena!

You are loved because of God's grace, not because of your performance. We love Him because He first loved us. God extended grace and mercy to us before we ever knew He existed. Your performance does not qualify you to be His child, called by His name. You receive His grace and love through faith, and that never changes. Your performance does not change His love for you, and His grace and mercy are held out to you continually as you toddle through the growth process.

Results of Personal Identity Valleys

What are the results of personal identity valleys into which we fall?

Stubbornness and dogmatism. This happens not because the prophetic person is rebellious or wicked, but because he or she is trying to survive! Our aim is not survival, however, but death to self.

Extravagant deliveries. When you are trying to survive, the claim of "thus saith the Lord" gets louder and more emotional with every delivery. Simplicity is thrown out the window and self-promotion becomes the norm.

An unteachable spirit. "I hear from God, and I learn from no one!" Have you ever heard that one? We are members of a local body because God knew we needed each other to fulfill our destiny in Him. We will always need the Body of Christ.

Valley #4: Guilt by Association

Have you ever fallen into the valley of guilt by association? You think you are doing okay, when suddenly a list of bad comments about some group you are associated with pops up out of nowhere. As far as you know, you have not done any of those things. Then someone points a finger at you and says, "You are one of *those people,* aren't you?" What is your reaction? Do you want to hide and say, "Who, me?"

We can learn a lot from the life of Peter concerning guilt by association. After he claimed boldly that he would never forsake the Lord, Jesus was arrested. Peter followed Him at a distance into the courtyard of the high priest's home where Jesus had been taken for questioning. Peter tried hard to stay loyal to the Lord. But when people began to associate him openly with Jesus, embarrassment, shame and fear suddenly raised their ugly heads, and Peter stumbled headlong into the valley of guilt by association.

First, people made statements (quoted in Luke 22) about Peter's identity:

"This man was with Him too." (verse 56)

"You are one of them too!" (verse 58)

"Certainly this man also was with Him, for he is a Galilean too." (verse 59)

Peter denied not only his Lord but also his own identity:

"Woman, I do not know Him." (verse 57)

"Man, I am not!" (verse 58)

"Man, I do not know what you are talking about." (verse 60)

"The Lord turned and looked at Peter. And Peter remembered the word of the Lord, how He had told him, 'Before a rooster crows today, you will deny Me three times.' And he went out and wept bitterly" (verses 61–62). Can you imagine the pain Peter must have felt when Jesus, his Lord and friend, turned and looked deeply into his soul? That glance must have cut through to the core of his being and divided spirit and soul. Peter was in a very dark valley, in the throes of death to self.

God wants to heal that pain, but He also wants to us to die. The devil and God have one thing in common: They are both out to kill us!

If you have ever experienced the fame and glory that come with the name of Christ, it is a sign that you are authentic. When people see evidence that you are associated with Jesus, it means there is something real about your message or lifestyle. But the pointing finger of accusation and the reactions you may feel can cause real pain. It is a time to die to self and be identified with the sufferings of Christ.

The pain of denial is much worse than the pain of being associated with Jesus and those who follow Him. You may have done nothing wrong, but persecution is a very real part of following Christ.

Valley #5: Revelation without Compassion

The valley of anger is another common trap that awaits prophetic people. The story of Jonah gives us an excellent picture of an angry prophet.

Jonah had a great problem. The word of the Lord had come to him to go and prophesy to Nineveh. But because Ninevites were notorious for their atrocities against the Hebrew people, Jonah probably hated them. Can you imagine what it might feel like if God gave you a word that He was going to pour out His mercy on someone who had given you a lot of grief? That would be a hard word to give.

The prophet fled and jumped right into the valley of anger. He did not have the heart of God and did not really want it. Even after his obedience to give the word of the Lord to Nineveh, and after its repentance, he held on to his anger (see Jonah 4:3–4).

Years ago I was part of a fellowship in Kansas City that came under some persecution and criticism from another ministry that had blessed me personally. I grew angry over the situation. I felt caught between these two groups, since I had been nurtured by both. I have never tasted anger such as I did then. I was hurt and confused by the reactions on both sides.

During the midst of that turbulent time, Mike Bickle, the senior leader of the team I was part of, talked openly about his own anger and the wisdom God had given him. The Lord revealed to him that the degree of his own anger was the degree of his own ambition. What a measuring stick! And did I ever have to check my heart on that one!

God gives us revelation, and then we face situations, like this one with Jonah, in which He instantly plumbs the depths of our sin-sick souls. His words and acts of mercy toward others can expose the amount of unforgiveness and lack of mercy in our own souls.

Jonah continued to wallow in anger and took a spot above the city to watch and see what God would do. God had mercy on him by providing a shade plant, keeping him from the discomfort of the heat of the sun. Jonah was happy with the plant. But then the Lord sent a worm to eat it up, and Jonah was exposed to the elements.

> When the sun came up God appointed a scorching east wind, and the sun beat down on Jonah's head so that he became faint and begged with all his soul to die, saying, "Death is better to me than life." Then God said to Jonah, "Do you have good reason to be angry about the plant?" And he said, "I have good reason to be angry, even to death." Then the LORD said, "You had compassion on the plant for which you did not work and which you did not cause to grow, which came up overnight and perished overnight. Should I not have compassion on Nineveh, the great city in which there are more than 120,000 persons who do not know the difference between their right and left hand, as well as many animals?"
>
> Jonah 4:8–11

God's compassion extended even to the dumb animals of that city. He wanted to reveal to Jonah the depth of compassion and mercy lacking in his own life. Jonah's heart was hard and God's mercy exposed it, but in the process God saved a whole city from destruction for another 110 years.

God will use all the circumstances in our lives to reveal Himself and expose our hearts so that we can be changed "from glory to glory" (2 Corinthians 3:18), or may I say from "gory to glory." He exposes the "gory" places of our hearts and, through repentance and forgiveness, changes them to "glory" places where He can bring His mercy and compassion. So we go from gory to glory and from glory to glory.

We must move away from the Old Testament prophetic stereotype with the loud voice, pointed finger and hard, judgmental attitude. One of the necessary ingredients in prophetic maturation is cultivating a heart of compassion.

Valley #6: Ditches on Both Sides to Avoid

Here are some attitudes and reactions to avoid on both sides of the street as they, too, will send you into a dark valley:

- People treat you special.
- People quit treating you special.
- People want to wind you up like a toy and get you to prophesy on demand.
- You are not prepared but are called "up front" to prophesy.
- You are ready but nothing comes.
- You are ready but you are not called on.
- You are ready but nobody wants it, likes it or responds to it.
- You make messes for yourself and others to clean up.
- There are so many parameters in place that you are afraid to do anything.
- You are afraid to risk your reputation.
- You have exaggerated a word and everyone knows it.
- You have exaggerated a word and no one knows it except you and God.
- Your gift exceeds your character. Woe!

These might sound a bit humorous, but most people do not laugh much when it happens to them.

Draw Near to His Throne of Grace

So, how many of these valleys hit home with you? It is so important to remember that our loving Father offers a way out of all these and other valleys you will walk through on your prophetic journey. Because of this, "Let us draw near with confidence to the throne of grace, so that we may receive mercy and find grace to help in time of need" (Hebrews 4:16).

Hosea prophesied the following:

> "Come, let us return to the LORD. For He has torn us, but He will heal us; He has wounded us, but He will bandage us. He will revive us after two days; He will raise us up on the third day that we may live before Him. So let us know, let us press on to know the LORD. His going forth is as certain as the dawn; and He will come to us like the rain, like the spring rain watering the earth."
>
> Hosea 6:1–3

This is a prophetic word about the Messiah—His death, burial and resurrection. But it is also a message for the people of the Messiah, the Body of Christ. It is a comforting word of God's grace and mercy toward us as we experience the peaks and valleys of a prophetic lifestyle.

There will be times of wounding and dying to selfish ambition, but our Father promises hope and help for those who are weary. He has not left us alone in the battle to perish. The Holy Spirit will come and bind us up and resurrect the prophetic graces He has imparted, so we can continue to fight the good fight with the strength and power of His grace, and with His merciful hand leading us on to victory. Be encouraged in your journey, and give away the valuable lessons you learn to those who are coming along behind you. Impart His presence to all those He gives you.

⟹ P R A Y E R ⟸

Lord Jesus, I need You. I have fallen into valleys that are dark and discouraging. But You are my light and my salvation, and You are the strength of my life. I pray, Father, lead me not into temptation, but deliver me from evil. Grant me grace and wisdom to avoid these valleys, yet walk through each valley with me in courage and strength. Shine the light of Your countenance upon me. Help me to learn from my past and be changed from glory to glory in response to the upward call in Christ Jesus. Amen.

⧈ Embracing Your Calling—Day 13

1. What are some of the prophetic valleys you have encountered?

2. How have you handled them? Have you been able to come out the other side in a better place, going from "glory to glory"?

3. From observing the experiences of others, what are some wisdom lessons that have given you insight?

4. Look at any recurring valleys in your life—those that show up consistently. Ask the Lord for wisdom and insight on how to handle these situations so they are no longer a stumbling block but become a testimony of God's faithfulness.

Avoiding the Snares

Church history is full of reports of anointed leaders who rose quickly to prominence only to become shooting stars, falling from their places of influence in front of the eyes of many who painfully observed their downward spiral. Ambition, immorality and other sins have caused the world to mock the Church as we have been less than adequate representatives of Christ on earth.

Jesus said that we are to "be shrewd as serpents and innocent as doves" (Matthew 10:16). But when we persistently, knowingly allow mixture of righteousness and unrighteousness in our lives, we open ourselves eventually to deception.

Let's begin this reading by looking at deceptions about the anointing. I will then share ways you can avoid these snares as you seek to embrace God's call on your life.

Samson: The Deception of the Anointing

Samson is a classic example of a person anointed by God who fell into the trap of deception. In just four chapters in the book of Judges, we find some peculiar and significant keys to understanding the anointing and the ways of God with people. Samson, one of the judges, was misled into a pattern of immorality while yet able to minister under the anointing, resulting in a swirl of chaos that only God can redeem (which He does, thank the Lord!).

We read in Judges that the Spirit of God would move on him suddenly, and an unusual anointing of strength would come on him to subdue the Philistines, the enemies of God's people. There was a mysterious secret to Samson's anointing: the length of his hair. Not cutting it was an outward prophetic representation of his inward vow of being consecrated to the Lord as a Nazirite.

You can imagine how the Philistines felt about this strong man of God. But Satan devised a nasty game plan to pull him down. The devil has strategies and tricks up his sleeve that are always loaded with corruption.

Samson's Tumble into the Gutter

Judges 16:1 depicts the scene graphically: "Samson went to Gaza and saw a harlot there, and went in to her." What was going on here? (Have you ever asked that question when one of God's anointed has fallen?) More than likely the enemy had been doing a study on Samson's manly weakness. He was apparently turning away from his inward vow of consecration and now wanted the best of both worlds—the realm of the Spirit and the realm of the flesh.

As Samson started to play around with the precious things of God, the "deception of the anointing" began to settle in and have its effect. ("I must be special; I can do anything I want.") But notice that God did not remove His gift from Samson. This is one of the bizarre things, and this is where the principle as found in Romans 11:29 comes into play: "The gifts and the calling of God are irrevocable."

Seemingly Samson got away with playing around. But the issue here is not the immediate outcome; rather, it is the long-term consequences of his actions. Ask yourself, *Where will the re-sults of my actions lead me a year from now? Five years from now?* Samson's Achilles' heel—a small but potentially mortal vulnerability—was now openly exposed, and the enemy was going to get him there if he could.

Samson's Enemies Set a Trap

Seemingly out of nowhere Delilah appeared on the scene and Samson loved her (see Judges 16:4). So the Philistines wove a conspiracy of sexual intrigue, paying off Delilah to coax out the secret to Samson's great strength.

"Delilah said to Samson, 'Please tell me where your great strength is and how you may be bound to afflict you'" (Judges 16:6).

Excuse me, but can you see the scene? The enemy's camp was following the plot. The woman seduced her way right into his face, wearing who knows what, just to destroy the man of God. Do you think she really cared about Samson? She was in it for what she could get—eleven hundred pieces of silver from each of the lords of the Philistines (see verse 5).

Probably Samson was thinking, *The last time they bound me, I snapped the cords and then took a jawbone and killed a thousand men. I'll just play along with her little game. After all, I'm indestructible. I'm God's anointed.*

So as Delilah persisted in her question, Samson, playing a little closer to the edge of the cliff, wove a tale of where his secret lay: If he was bound with "seven fresh cords" (verse 7), he would lose his strength. She tied him up with these and set the Philistines on him. Again the strength of God was released, and Samson triumphed over what seemed a trivial escapade. But the woman would not give up.

So it is in our day. Give the devil an inch and he will take a mile. Never give the seducer the time of day.

Without realizing it, Samson was beginning to get worn down. As he weakened, Delilah got a little closer to knowing the truth of his strength. He concocted tales starting with seven fresh cords, then "new ropes" (verse 11), and then—slipping a bit—said, "If you weave the seven locks of my hair" into the web of the loom, "then I will become weak and be like any other man" (verse 13). At this point, speaking about his hair, he was flirting around with his secret.

The Philistines failed once again to capture him, so the seductress really turned on the charm: "How can you say, 'I love you,' when your heart is not with me?" (verse 15). The demonic power encounter was now turned up to level ten. "It came about when she pressed him daily with her words and urged him, that his soul was annoyed to death" (verse 16). Beaten down, Samson finally spilled the beans. What difference did it make? He was still God's anointed. "He told her all that was in his heart" (verse 17), the secret to his strength.

Delilah lured him into her lap, lulled him to sleep and had a man shave off his seven locks of hair. Sure enough, they got their payoff: "His strength left him" (verse 19). When the Philistines came in to get him, Samson assumed he would shake them off as before. But he had played one time too many with the devil's fire. Listen to these ominous words of Scripture: "He did not know that the Lord had departed from him" (verse 20).

Captured by the enemy, Samson was tortured and his eyes were put out. Now he was just another backslidden, natural, tormented man. God's destiny had evaded him as he became a grain grinder in a Philistine prison. What a tragic state of affairs!

The Results of Losing Your Strength

The sad thing is, whole denominations, ministries, movements, congregations and individuals find themselves in the same state of affairs. All that remains is a mere skeleton and shadow of the authentic creation God called them to be. When wisdom is not the guardian of the anointing, drastic results may occur, as they did with Samson.

- He lost his hair, his strength, his joy—the loss of covering and protection.
- He lost his sight—the absence of prophetic revelation and vision.
- He lost his function, left to grind grain at the prison mill—the torment of lost destiny and purpose.

I have long since seen too much—everything from senior pastors running off with their secretaries, to evangelists becoming beguiled by the "I-am-special" syndrome, to cultish exclusivity due to the pride of a supposed prophet's revelation. (You can add to the list.) Such lapses are expected in the world. The problem is, the worldly system is in the Church.

Enough is enough! It is time for a revolution of lifestyle that will restore the radical roots of the Church. It is time to wake up from sleeping in Delilah's lap and escape while we can. Oh, may a holy deliverance come forth to cleanse the Bride of Christ!

The Mercy of God at Work

In the midst of it all, mercy was at work in Samson's life. "The hair of his head began to grow again after it was shaved off" (verse 22). Praise the Lord! Yes, I said, Praise the Lord! Thank the Lord for the recovery and restoration of any individual or ministry. Do whatever you can to help restore a fallen brother or sister (see Galatians 6:1–3). Your attitude and response to his or her condition might just determine your own next level of grace, promotion or demotion.

It is not over till it is over. The Philistines, celebrating in the temple of Dagon, called for their prime-time prisoner to entertain them (see Judges 16:25). Little did they know, he was no longer bald and weak. I think he had learned some lessons in his prison cell concerning the fear of the Lord, and about correctly handling the gifts of God.

"Samson called to the LORD and said, 'O Lord GOD, please remember me and please strengthen me just this time, O God, that I may at once be avenged of the Philistines for my two eyes'" (verse 28). His final act of power and ministry was fulfilled as he pulled on the two middle pillars, and the whole building came crashing down, crushing three thousand Philistine men and women—and Samson himself.

Yes, he was restored to his calling. But what a high price to pay, and what a poor way to end up—sacrificing his own life. Thank the Lord for His merciful heart, as Samson's strength returned, and along with it a measure of his purpose and calling. The Lord did triumph over His enemies.

Every individual, like Samson, has a special gift from God (see 1 Peter 4:10–11), a special way the supernatural presence of God works with and through him or her. But, like Samson, each gifted person also has a distinct place of vulnerability (see 1 Corinthians 10:13–14). But those places of weakness, when surrendered to the Lord, can become the very mechanisms that keep you in humility and connectedness with our Messiah. Your weakness will either become the place where the enemy beguiles you, or else the place where God's power is perfected in you. The choice is yours.

When Deception Settles In

Deception trickles in when people draw up false equations of *why* they are anointed. When you think you deserve the anointing, that you earned this special grace, that special treatment is owed you as the man or woman of God, then self-justification has captured you, and deception is close at hand.

Sexual Issues and the Anointing

The following truths pertain to young and old, male and female, married and single. Ministering in the anointing of the Holy Spirit is a real rush. You can become so caught up in the Spirit that everything natural temporarily fades into the background. Even natural, physiological desires and appetites seem to be put on pause. You are engaged with God. It is heavenly! The power is flowing. The divine intelligence of the Holy Spirit seems to be flying around the room, available for everyone to capture. His awesome presence is among us!

But when the ministry engagement is over, the anointing gradually wears off and you are left a hunk of flesh, just like the next person. It seemed as if you were changed into another person in the anointing, a very spiritual person, but now you are a physical creature altogether. Ouch! Fatigue, tiredness and appetites all come to visit. Sometimes loneliness hits people who are anointed by God, and times of greater vulnerability and spiritual warfare hit them after direct ministry engagement. Instead of those sexual appetites lessening, now they are building up. Apparently they were only put on hold.

The enemy has a trap for you, just as he did for Samson. What is it?

The Eye Gate

In his book *The Prophetic Ministry* Rick Joyner gives some good old-fashioned fatherly advice: "We can let either light or darkness into our soul through our eyes. If we are going to function as eyes for the Lord's body, we must give our eyes to Him, to be used only for His holy purposes. We must not let darkness into our soul through what we allow ourselves to look at. Lust is one of the primary destroyers of prophetic vision. Lust is selfishness in its basest form—the exact opposite of the nature of the Lord, whom we are seeking to emulate."[1]

If we in prophetic ministry are to be considered the eyes of the Body (see Isaiah 29:10), then we must lead the way by calling for cleansing of the eyes and guarding of the eye gate. We need to make a covenant with our eyes so that our vision will be clear (see Job 31:1; Luke 11:34).

Exaltation and Worship of Human Vessels

I was once given a stunning dream depicting plausible reasons for the failures of three spiritual leaders who had large followings regionally and nationally. Each situation was distinctly different. But the enemy struck them in the place of their Achilles' heels. The problems, as depicted in my dream, centered around:

1. *Exaltation of position.* This resulted in the soulish manipulating, pushing and pressuring of others. The heart of a bully was more at work than the character of the Lamb. In contrast, we are to function for the purpose of servanthood. We wage war with a sword in the heavenlies but with a towel on earth.

2. *Exaltation of revelation.* This resulted in a profuse display of giftedness as people became addicted to getting "words," and the gifted one became addicted to the attention of giving words. No gift is to overshadow the main and plain devotion to the Scriptures. The revelatory is to complement, not compete with, the Word of God.

3. *Exaltation of interpretation.* This resulted in the elevation of one's personal interpretation as higher than that of others. Elitism crept in. Pride set in. Then new doctrines were formed out of the concept that these leaders were special—the elect ones! There is no private interpretation of Scripture. We must walk with others and avoid elitism and isolationism from the larger Body of Christ.

When the Hand of God Is Lifted

I was given another vivid, wisdom-filled dream in which I was shown three things that can occur when the hand of God is lifted off a man or woman. God's hand brings protection, covering, blessing and giftedness. But due to persistent sin, disobedience or other issues, God might lift His hand off a person for a season. This seems to be what happened with Samson, through sin: God's hand lifted and Samson was not aware of it.

In this dream I saw three things that will try to come and camp out at your doorstep if you do not run to Him during your time of testing:

1. The issue you have struggled with in private becomes more difficult, and it is sometimes revealed or exposed in public.

2. The thing you have feared in the past becomes drawn to you like a magnet.

3. The desire for former sinful habits (weaknesses, compulsions or obsessions) escalates.

Triumphs are now about to become tragedies.

After I woke up from this dream, the fear of the Lord came on me (may it also come on you!), and I cried out to the Lord, "O God, I am dependent on Your hand of protection. May Your hand never lift off me. May I never give You a reason that Your hand would have to lift off my life—for my family's sake and for Your holy name's sake. Help, Lord!"

I encourage you to lift an authentic, heartfelt prayer and commit the conduct of your life to Him.

Trust the Holy Spirit

You can trust the Holy Spirit. He is the one who anoints us and comes to make Jesus into a living reality. The Spirit is the gift of the Father sent to empower us to be victorious over the kingdom of darkness.

In this section we have looked at a lifestyle of wisdom—the incredible revelatory storehouse God has provided; wise principles concerning revelatory gifts that will help us to release the counsel of God correctly with understanding; peaks and valleys of a prophetic lifestyle; and snares we can avoid if we will use the wisdom of the Holy Spirit.

Some use our very real need to get wisdom as an excuse for not stepping out in faith. But I want to encourage your heart and motivate you on to love and to good works. The enemy wants to magnify the mistakes of the past, as well as the weaknesses of others and ourselves, and turn them into tools of fear. But "God has not given us a spirit of timidity, but of power and love and discipline" (2 Timothy 1:7). Let's learn wisdom, but let's also get up and do some damage to the darkness in Jesus' name.

⟹ P R A Y E R ⟸

Father, forgive me for any way I have treated Your spiritual tools as toys. Show me areas of sin or points of weakness that are hindering the move of Your Spirit in me and through me. Deliver me from any spirit of deception. Help me not be ignorant of the devil's schemes. Teach me wisdom so I can be a good steward of Your presence and power. Give me more of Your Holy Spirit. Anoint me with encounters of a heavenly kind. Lead me into truth and Your Kingdom ways. I ask that You would give me mentors who will help to be eyes for me. Teach me how to handle the precious gifts of God, that others will see the real Jesus. In His precious name I pray, Amen.

Embracing Your Calling—Day 14

1. What part of the story of Samson speaks to you most poignantly? Why?

2. What are some of the misconceptions that can deceive people concerning the issues of handling the anointing?

3. What are some practices you want to have in place to have a lifestyle of walking in the anointing over the long term?

4. Talk to the Lord about any recurring snares in which you find yourself consistently. Ask the Holy Spirit to reveal the root and a solution for you. Pursue whatever He says diligently and tell the Lord, "May I never give You a reason that Your hand would have to lift off my life."

The Lifestyle
of Revelation

So I prophesied as He commanded me, and the
breath came into them, and they came to life and
stood on their feet, an exceedingly great army.

EZEKIEL 37:10

Ezekiel—Prophet
of Visionary Revelation

Ezekiel—a Hebrew priest called to be a prophet—has evoked much interest in Judaism, Christianity and Islam. He even has struck a chord with modern ufologists, who claim that the extensive detail and design given in his visionary experiences are proof he was reporting a sighting of an extraterrestrial spacecraft. What Ezekiel saw was definitely out of this world, and he saw a being of a heavenly kind—God Himself.

Both Jeremiah and Daniel were contemporaries of Ezekiel. Jewish tradition has also advocated that Ezekiel counseled Hananiah, Mishael and Azariah (also called Shadrach, Meshach and Abednego) that they should resist Nebuchadnezzar's command and choose death in a fiery furnace rather than bow down to his golden image.

Little is known about Ezekiel's personal life. He was the son of Buzi and is presumed a descendant of the priestly family of Zadok. At the age of 25 he was among those who were exiled to Babylonia with King Jehoiachin in 597 BC or shortly thereafter.

Unlike Jeremiah, who remained single, Ezekiel had a wife whom he loved as "the desire of [his] eyes" (Ezekiel 24:16). There is no mention that they had any children; however, his wife died young, four years after Ezekiel had begun his prophetic ministry when he was just 34 years old.

Ezekiel's Call as a Prophet

When Ezekiel was thirty years old, he received his calling to be a prophet through a visionary revelation when "the heavens were opened and I saw visions of God" (Ezekiel 1:1).

After seeing four stunning, living beings, he then saw a radiant Man. The Man!

> Then I noticed from the appearance of His loins and upward something like glowing metal that looked like fire all around within it, and from the appearance of His loins and downward I saw something like fire; and there was a radiance around Him. As the appearance of the rainbow in the clouds on a rainy day, so was the appearance of the surrounding radiance. Such was the appearance of the likeness of the glory of the LORD. And when I saw it, I fell on my face and heard a voice speaking.
>
> Then He said to me, "Son of man, stand on your feet that I may speak with you!" As He spoke to me the Spirit entered me and set me on my feet; and I heard Him speaking to me. Then He said to me, "Son of man, I am sending you to the sons of Israel, to a rebellious people who have rebelled against Me; they and their fathers have transgressed against Me to this very day. I am sending you to them who are stubborn and obstinate children, and you shall say to them, 'Thus says the Lord GOD.' As for them, whether they listen or not—for they are a rebellious house—they will know that a prophet has been among them. And you, son of man, neither fear them nor fear their words, though thistles and thorns are with you and you sit on scorpions;

neither fear their words nor be dismayed at their presence, for they are a rebellious house."

Ezekiel 1:27–2:6

And so Ezekiel's prophetic ministry began. What a way to begin! Ezekiel's prophetic ministry occurred during the darkest hour in Old Testament history—the seven years preceding the 586 BC destruction of Jerusalem and the fifteen years following it. His prophetic ministry had a threefold purpose:

1. To deliver God's message of judgment to apostate Judah and Jerusalem and to the seven nations around her.
2. To sustain the faith of God's remnant in exile concerning the restoration of His covenant people and the final glory of His Kingdom.
3. To make each person aware of his or her own responsibility to God. The exilic judgment was not simply the result of their ancestors' sins.

Ezekiel 9:9 summarizes how completely corrupt Jerusalem had become in its last decade, as the Lord spoke to Ezekiel: "The iniquity of the house of Israel and Judah is very, very great, and the land is filled with blood and the city is full of perversion; for they say, 'The Lord has forsaken the land, and the Lord does not see!'"

Into this setting came Ezekiel. He lived a lifestyle of revelation and called Israel to turn to the Lord, warned of coming judgment, which he lived to see personally, and foretold the restoration of Israel back to their land.

The setting many of us live in today is no different. The iniquity around us, including in the Church, is great. Our land is filled with blood and our cities are full of perversion. People do not fear God because they do not believe He sees or exists. Sin is bold and even flaunted.

Let's look at what Ezekiel saw and see how he responded to revelation from God. We can receive instruction from this example so that we take heed and do not fall ourselves (see 1 Corinthians 10:11–12).

What Did Ezekiel See?

Ezekiel recorded more visionary experiences than any other prophet in the Old Testament. Let's look at some of these visionary experiences.

Glory of God (Ezekiel 1:3, 12–14, 23)

We have already looked at the glorious vision of Ezekiel that launched him into his call as a prophet. What amazes me about this passage is how long Ezekiel continued to look into this vision. How often when the Lord shows us something through a revelatory gift or in Scripture do we get up immediately or quickly go tell someone? Ezekiel's intentional and prolonged gaze got him more than a word: It brought him into the presence of the Radiant One. The lesson to learn here is to *keep looking* into the vision God gives you. Jesus desires to enlighten the eyes of your heart and encounter you (see Ephesians 1:17–19). Keep looking!

Vision of the Scroll (Ezekiel 2:10; 3:3)

"Then I looked, and behold, a hand was extended to me; and lo, a scroll was in it. . . . He said to me, 'Son of man, feed your stomach and fill your body with this scroll which I am giving you'" (Ezekiel 2:9; 3:3). God then told Ezekiel that He was sending him to his own people—people who should listen to him, but would not because they did not want to listen to God Himself (3:6–7). Sounds like what Jesus experienced: "He came to His own, and those who were His own did not receive Him" (John 1:11). It was as though God was warning Ezekiel that "no prophet is welcome in his hometown" (Luke 4:24).

Still God said to Ezekiel, "Go to the exiles, to the sons of your people, and speak to them and tell them, whether they listen or not" (Ezekiel 3:11). May the vision of His words and the Word Himself sustain us and provide strength to speak the truth in love with conviction, whether those we speak to listen or not. Give us ears to hear, O Lord!

Man of Fire and Coals of Fire (Ezekiel 8; 10)

The Lord also showed Ezekiel the terrible abominations being practiced back at the Jerusalem Temple and the destruction the Lord was about to send upon the city. When Ezekiel saw the judgments striking down the people, he did not say, "That's right, God. Get 'em. They deserve that much and even more." Old Testament prophets have long been branded as men with strong words and hard hearts. But Ezekiel's heart was far from hard as he fell on his face and cried out saying, "Alas, Lord GOD! Are You destroying the whole remnant of Israel by pouring out Your wrath on Jerusalem?" (Ezekiel 9:8).

After Ezekiel saw the glory of the Lord depart from the Temple, the Lord instructed him to prophesy against the leaders "who devise iniquity and give evil advice in this city" (11:2). As he was prophesying, one of the leaders died right in front of him. Yikes! What was Ezekiel's response? The same as before. He "fell on [his] face and cried out with a loud voice and said, 'Alas, Lord GOD! Will You bring the remnant of Israel to a complete end?'" (11:13).

The lesson to learn here is one of compassion and mercy. Ezekiel did not prophesy judgment because he was disgusted or just plain angry at the people. He spoke to the people because of what he saw and what he was told to speak. This is to be our method as well: to prophesy what we see and hear while maintaining a heart of compassion and mercy, since God is not willing that any should perish but wants all to come to repentance (see 2 Peter 3:9).

Valley of Dry Bones (Ezekiel 37:1–14)

We will take a look at this visionary experience in detail in the reading for Day 20. As Ezekiel responded to the vision and *prophesied life*, he saw a future day when God would raise His people up and bring them back into the land of Israel. As we will see, our role is to prophesy to the breath and bring forth the Spirit of God where death has been ruling.

Jerusalem and the Temple (Ezekiel 40–48)

Ezekiel was fifty years old when the Lord showed him what is sometimes called the "Millennial Temple" that Jesus will build after His Second Coming, which will become the seat of His earthly government during the Millennial Kingdom (see Zechariah 6:12–13). What a marvelous vision that the Church still is longing to see come to pass!

River Flowing from the Temple (Ezekiel 47:1–12)

Read this beautiful vision of hope and life from Ezekiel 47:9–12:

It will come about that every living creature which swarms in every place *where the river goes, will live*. And there will be very many fish, for *these waters go there and the others become fresh; so everything will live where the river goes*. And it will come about that fishermen will stand beside it; from Engedi to Eneglaim there will be a place for the spreading of nets. Their fish will be according to their kinds, like the fish of the Great Sea, very many. But its swamps and marshes will not become fresh; they will be left for salt. By the river on its bank, on one side and on the other, will grow *all kinds of trees for food. Their leaves will not wither and their fruit will not fail.* They will *bear every month because their water flows from the sanctuary,* and their *fruit will be for food and their leaves for healing.*

emphasis added

This prophecy refers to real events that have yet to take place probably concerning natural Israel. It also has many applications to us today as the Body of Christ that is a devotional reading in and of itself. Ezekiel saw a river flowing from the house of God bringing life to everything that touches it. This vision must capture our hearts so that we "jump into the river" ourselves and bring healing and life to the nations. Are you flowing in the river of God?

What Did Ezekiel Do?

Ezekiel was not a prophet who got to speak cool prophetic words that made people feel good about themselves. Nor did he receive awards for his foreknowledge. Nor was anyone at the local art store asking for color prints of his visions.

I am not sure why anyone would aspire to be a prophet if he or she were only to look at the lives and lifestyles of the prophets in the Bible—experiencing loneliness, rejection, persecution and execution; eating strange things; wearing uncomfortable clothing or no clothing at all in public for long periods of time; not getting married or marrying a prostitute who continued to be unfaithful; getting swallowed by a whale and trying to survive in the dark with half-digested fish for three days; having to do strange, uncommon prophetic acts to make a statement; and the list continues.

So are you sure you want to be a prophet or even live a prophetic lifestyle? Let me give you a hint: The true prophet is at a crosscurrent with society, challenges others to be like Jesus, carries a tailor-made cross and dies daily to self!

We have seen that Ezekiel was exiled and taken into captivity. His wife died early in their marriage. The people did not listen to what he had to say. He had to prophesy against his own city, and then saw that prophecy fulfilled. I do not believe that Ezekiel let out a sigh of relief, thankful his word came to pass. I believe he was deeply grieved by the loss of the land promised to his forefather Abraham.

The lifestyle of a prophet sounds like a blast, right? Not always, at least looking at it from this point of view. Yet those who are called to live a prophetic life continue to walk their unique paths toward the upward calling of God in Christ.

So what did Ezekiel do in response to what he saw and heard? Ezekiel 40:4 describes the request of the Lord: "Son of man, *see* with your eyes, *hear* with your ears, and *give attention* to all that I am going to show you; for you have been brought here in order to show it to you. *Declare* to the house of Israel all that you see" (emphasis added). This verse highlights our response: to see, hear, give attention and then declare.

Ezekiel kept looking to see what God wanted to show him. He ate the word and spoke His Word, even when no one was listening; he kept a heart of mercy and compassion in the midst of delivering at times very difficult words to his own people who were rebellious and refused to listen; he prophesied to the breath and saw the dead come back to life; he saw the restoration of the house of God and the river of God give life to all that touched it.

We, too, can follow in this devoted lifestyle of revelation. Some see dry bones but the clear prophet will keep looking until he or she sees an army!

The Lifestyle of Revelation

There are different paths for each person to receive revelation. Do you prefer to ride an elevator, or at least an escalator, or do you always seem to take the stairs? What does this have to do with prophetic revelation?

Some profoundly gifted people, it seems, just get onto an elevator and the operator says, "What floor?" These people respond, "Well, the top, of course!" And the next thing they know, they are on the rooftop with a panoramic view of the whole city. Talk about dreams and visions—they are there! They are not exactly sure how they got there, but what does it matter? The overnight delivery package has arrived and they have taken a quantum leap into the Spirit realm.

Other people are stair steppers. In their gift development they take one step at a time—step by step by hard step. They hear the stories of the others whom God has called up hither, and they begin to wither! By the time they have climbed the first few flights of stairs, with much perspiration, they are beginning to wonder, *Where was I when they handed out work assignments? Did I miss my true calling?*

God has His reasoning, and His ways are not our ways. There is the sovereignty of God and then there is our cooperation with His calling. Both factors always come into play. I have observed the following simple points in this mix of elevator-riders versus stair-climbers that have helped me in my pilgrimage.

The Elevator Riders

- A sovereign gift; like Jeremiah, they are born with it or like Ezekiel the Lord calls them through a dramatic, visionary experience
- Early operation, even though they may not be walking closely with God

- Anointing often greater than their training; great experiences but sometimes lack wisdom in their operation of it
- Sensitive in their emotional makeup
- Can suffer from an increased amount of rejection and isolation
- Can be tempted to think too highly of themselves—that they are special
- Not typically good teachers, as they do not know how they got what they have
- Need to cultivate humility and gratitude

The Staircase Climbers

- Develop slowly and progressively; gift does not appear overnight; they can even be late bloomers
- Proceed one step at a time, like climbing a mountain
- Progress through faithfulness
- Can suffer from intimidation and even jealousy
- Must avoid the "if-only" thoughts
- Prone toward a works mentality and self-righteousness: "I deserve this; I earned it!"
- Should continue in faithfulness and endurance while cultivating a revelation of God's grace

Regardless of how you receive your call, a life of revelation is a part of the lifestyle of a prophet or those who are prophetic. Generally this is what people think of when considering what it means to be a prophet—receiving revelatory experiences and delivering God's words to people. While this is true, it is imperative that the revelation be grounded in both a lifestyle of intimacy and wisdom, which is why "The Lifestyle of Revelation" is the third section in this book and not the first. As you explore the lifestyle of revelation, remain mindful of the content and heart in the previous two sections.

In this last section, we are going to explore a lifestyle of revelation, which will include learning how to collaborate with others in the Kingdom in our revelation, learning to unite with others of diverse giftings, seizing your prophetic destiny, growing in revelation, prophesying life and embracing a new paradigm for living a prophetic lifestyle in the 21st century. Buckle up as we jump on our prophetic chariot and gaze into the ultimate revelation of the glorious Man, Christ Jesus.

⟩ P R A Y E R ⟨

Lord Jesus, we want to see you. You are truly magnificent and glorious. Open the heavens and open my eyes to see visions of God. Bring me into Your awesome presence where I can look upon your beauty and majesty. As I look upon the multitudes, fill my heart with compassion and release Your healing through me. There is a river of life flowing out of me! Holy Spirit, bring life to everyone I touch. Father God, as I read this next section, I ask for an increase in revelatory understanding and gifting that I may walk in a lifestyle of revelation. Work in me that which is well pleasing in Your sight. For Jesus' sake, Amen.

⧎ Embracing Your Calling—Day 15

1. Consider the profound nature of what Ezekiel saw. Choose one of the visions and make personal application for yourself today.

2. Ezekiel was a prophet of *visionary* revelation. Have you experienced visions? How do you typically receive revelation?

3. Has your prophetic journey been more like an elevator or the stairs? Explain.

4. Reflect on Ezekiel's lifestyle of revelation and the response he received. Read Ezekiel 40:4 and ask the Lord to help you see, hear, give attention and then declare what He gives you.

Kingdom Collaboration

Division within the ranks of the Church throughout history has caused numerous casualties and great separation within the Body of Christ. Today a clarion call is sounding from the heart of the Father for all parts of the Body of Christ to work together as a lifestyle. When opposites attract, a new birth occurs. Let's cry out for healing, reconciliation and collaboration to arise.

In today's reading we will examine some of the reasons for the misunderstandings that have led to unrest and animosity within the Body of Christ. There is room for change and correction, and the Holy Spirit is well able to facilitate this retraining for every believer with a willing heart. The Lord of hosts will not lead a dysfunctional army into battle!

Our Kingdom ATM

Around fifteen years ago I was given a dream that I have chewed on like a cow with its cud ever since. In fact, when I was awakened from the dream, I sighed and heard myself say, "Now that would be a dream!" It was a dream that I want to see come into being with my very own eyes.

In my dream I was pointing to a leader and prophesying to him. These words were very clear: "It's time for the A-Team. It's time for the ATM. It's time for the authentic *apostolic team ministry* to begin. It will be apostolic—authentic, abandoned Christianity. It will be telescopic—the prophets looking through the lens of time and the evangelists telling the Good News. It will be microscopic—the pastors and administrators caring for the flock of God."

As I awoke from the dream—which appeared to emphasize genuine relationship rather than structural authority—I was catapulted into an open vision in which I took a key card and inserted it into an ATM banking device. Cash started pouring out. A supply of finances beyond my dreams was now available.

As I pondered the vision, I realized that when two or three come into agreement (see Matthew 18:19), they will use the ATM card of the Kingdom of God, asking in prayer for heavenly withdrawals from God's bank account to be released, in order to have ample supply to do whatever He wants done. The apostolic team ministry would have an abundant supply to equip the Church freely, so that she in turn could do the work of ministry (see Ephesians 4:11–13). Now that *would* be a dream!

As we understand the differences between the roles of revelatory gifting and of governmental leadership within the local church, we will learn to appreciate each role as equally vital and necessary to the health and soundness of the Body of Christ. There is only one Head and there is only one Body (with many parts) that serves the Head. We need one another to function and contribute fully as part of God's great army.

Let me emphasize, too, that when I speak of "government" in today's reading, I refer to the leadership within the local church, including the pastoral and apostolic ministries, and not necessarily secular government.

Foundational Collaboration Principles

The role of those who walk in a lifestyle of revelation is to stand in the council of God and then be an oracle or spokesman for Him. The prophetic part of the Body points the way, like a road sign, to the plan of God or to God Himself. The roles of governmental leadership within the Church (pastoral, apostolic and eldership) are to steward designated resources and responsibilities for God. They bring application into being.

These giftings and ministries diverge by definition but not purpose. They are both serving God's purposes. Sometimes the prophetic and governmental leadership of the Church have seemed to be at opposite poles. It has appeared to the world, to the Church and even to the Lord that they want nothing to do with each other. We need wisdom to honor one another, to cooperate together and to show one another mutual esteem.

Honor One Another

Jesus lives in each of us as believers, yet He does not give the whole meal deal to a single individual. That is why the Church is made up of *members* of the Body.

One individual may serve in a role (or grace) more proficiently than another, but never to the exclusion of that other person. We must learn to honor and discern the Body of Christ in order to receive the fullness of Christ.

One of the most strategic issues is honoring the spiritual fathers and mothers among us—and grandfathers and grandmothers, also. The joining of the generations occurs as this is done. The older must, in turn, bless the younger generations, becoming their coaches and best cheerleaders. Investing and honoring are keys to the move of God in His Body being continual and progressive rather than stagnant.

Cooperate

All ministries, offices and gifts, which are given to build up the Body of Christ, should function cooperatively, not in opposition to one another. "To each one is given the manifestation of the Spirit for the common good" (1 Corinthians 12:7; see also 1 Corinthians 14:12; Ephesians 4:11–16; 2 Timothy 3:16–17; 2 Peter 1:19–21). The Body is designed to function cooperatively. God has the idea that we need each other. Just try to go a day without using your thumbs, your sight or your legs. In the same way, when all parts of the Body of Christ demonstrate a lifestyle of collaboration "for the common good," the Kingdom of God makes significant forward movement.

Esteem One Another

Gifted individuals must find one another and operate in a context of mutual respect and esteem. Teaming with others is not only biblical, but it might just keep you from shipwreck. In recent years I have experienced great strength by associating with local, national and international councils in which mutual respect is a hallmark.

There is a saying that opposites attract. But in the Church that does not always ring true. Often the opposites repel each other and create great havoc. All too often we have pushed each other's sensitive buttons and repelled one another, diminishing the effectiveness of each of these vital parts of the Body.

God wants us to learn to appreciate the sensitivities of the gifting in each person and let His grace draw us together in the bond of love. By His wisdom and patience, we can learn how to move toward each other in mutual respect and esteem, and form a strong bond.

The Prophetic in Context of Leadership Community

Sometimes prophetic people put on eye masks and ride their horses in and out of town crying, "The Lone Ranger!" God has another idea.

What does the relationship of the prophetic and the community of believers look like? Where does the prophetic gifting fit into the everyday lives of the Church community? To get an idea, let's ponder some Scripture.

> You are no longer strangers and aliens, but you are fellow citizens with the saints, and are of God's household, having been built on the foundation of the apostles and prophets, Christ Jesus Himself being the corner stone, in whom the whole building, being fitted together, is growing into a holy temple in the Lord, in whom you also are being built together into a dwelling of God in the Spirit.
>
> Ephesians 2:19–22

The Church is one house under one Head, Jesus, with delegated responsibilities and spheres of authority. Do you believe that? Jesus does the delegating. He appoints whom He wants, where He wants.

From Outside the Camp . . .

Many times in the Old Testament, the prophetic operated from a position of isolation and alienation. When Israel persisted in rebellion, the Lord raised up voices from outside the camp to speak with hard words meant to prick the hearts and consciences of the leadership and community, and bring them to repentance and back to obedience.

Because of the alienation that occurs between the prophetically gifted and the community of believers as a whole, many still view the prophetic as a hard and critical ministry.

... To *Inside the Camp*

At other times in the Old Testament, and especially in the New Testament, God appointed voices from within the camp of believers to speak words that would bring encouragement and correction.

Even if a prophetic person speaks from outside the local community of believers, he or she may still have to deal with governmental leadership in order to clear up any misunderstandings and confusion related to the prophetic words. Does that not sound glorious! The point is, a relationship must be established in order for the prophetic ministry and the general community of believers to benefit from each other.

But the stereotype of the harsh prophetic voice is not the norm through which that gifting should function. We need a new lens to look through. Prophets are not anarchists fomenting rebellious revolution, but voices crying God's heart.

Contrasting Strengths

Remember that the purpose of both the prophetic and the governmental is for charging up the batteries of the everyday believer. Yes, I know the "governmental includes the prophet" but for this short review, let's consider the "governmental" as being more pastoral and apostolic. Let's look at the contrasting strengths found in each gift as tools we might use on a building site. The tools are quite different in function, but are used together to facilitate the construction of the building. Different grace tools are also used in different seasons or stages of the building process. (The contrasts here are generalized and not true in every instance.)

Prophetic	Governmental
subjective	objective
emotional	structural
more itinerant	more residential
functional	relational
intuitive	logical
idealistic	practical
more spontaneous	premeditative
personal	corporate
inspirational	informative
creative	managerial

Here are some Scriptures to explore that will shed more light on these contrasts: Matthew 16:3–19; Acts 20:17–38; 21:8–11; 2 Peter 1:19–21.

Here are more contrasts:

- The prophetic role is to hear and release the revelation of God.
- The governmental role is often to interpret the revelation and instruction of God and bring application to it.
- Without the prophetic, people become institutional, without life.
- Without the governmental, everyone does "what [is] right in his own eyes" (Judges 21:25).

Revelation without application means there is no receptacle present to contain and hold the revelatory content. Without a fresh wineskin, the new wine just spills onto the floor (see Matthew 9:17).

Understanding the contrasting strengths of the prophetic and governmental graces can give us new appreciation for the necessity to collaborate in the work of the Kingdom. Help, Lord, we need each other!

The Antioch Leadership Team

In gazing at this complex subject of Kingdom collaboration, let's take a closer look at a familiar Scripture about a meeting of first-century leaders at Antioch. As we ponder these verses, we will find a gold mine before us waiting to be excavated.

> There were at Antioch, in the church that was there, prophets and teachers: Barnabas, and Simeon who was called Niger, and Lucius of Cyrene, and Manaen who had been brought up with Herod the tetrarch, and Saul. While they were ministering to the Lord and fasting, the Holy Spirit said, "Set apart for Me Barnabas and Saul for the work to which I have called them." Then, when they had fasted and prayed and laid their hands on them, they sent them away.
>
> Acts 13:1–3

Who Were These Guys, Anyway?

For a moment I want to peer behind the scenes at these guys who got thrown together in this Antioch leadership prayer and fasting summit. You will be surprised at what we find.

BARNABAS, A MESSIANIC JEWISH PROPHET FROM CYPRUS

According to Acts 4:36, Barnabas's original name was Joseph. He was a Levite (that means he was a Jewish man preparing for the priesthood) who came from the island of Cyprus and met Jesus as his Messiah. The apostles called him *Barnabas*, which means "son of encouragement, exhortation or consolation." So here we have an islander Jew studying for the Levitical priesthood who met Jesus and became a messianic prophet.

SIMEON, A BLACK MAN

Next we find a convert named Niger. This term means "black man." Now imagine, we have a Jewish prophet and a black man whose national identity is not clearly revealed. But he was probably African, maybe Ethiopian. Interesting mix already!

Lucius, a Libyan Arab?

Lucius came to this summit from Cyrene, which was probably modern-day Libya. We do not know for sure, but Lucius could have been Arab in descent, coming from that part of northern Africa. Now this is starting to get volatile—a Jew, a black man and a north African, possibly an Arab. There was probably a whole lot of iron sharpening iron (see Proverbs 27:17) going on behind the scenes.

Manaen, the Greek Aristocrat

The name *Manaen* is Greek in origin. The text also says Manaen grew up with Herod the Ruler—the king who imprisoned John the Baptist and later beheaded him (Matthew 14:1–12). So Manaen, as a Greek aristocrat, had grown up with a whole different educational and philosophical worldview.

Saul, the Persecutor Convert from Tarsus

All the Acts passage says in identifying this man is "Saul." But by now all Luke's readers knew what this man had done—persecuted the Church, dragged men and women off to prison, carried out death threats. Was his zeal ever misdirected! We also know that Saul came from Tarsus, which would be in modern Turkey. Barnabas went on a mission to search out this revolutionary convert and bring him to Antioch to convene with the other leaders (see Acts 11:19–26).

How Could They Get Along?

Talk about a catfight—they could have been scratching one another's eyeballs out! They might still have been carrying some of the extra baggage that came with all of their ethnic, cultural, religious, political, philosophical, educational, preconceived, prideful, prejudicial thinking. In fact, I am sure of it. I think they were excited about this historic summit and probably more than a bit apprehensive at the same time. How would they get along?

Realize, too, that the Scriptures indicate these five men even came with opposite giftings. Two or three of them were teachers and the other two or three were noted prophets. From my experience, that alone was a miracle, since it is extraordinary for prophets and teachers to complement, bless, honor and esteem one another. God had His work cut out for Him! They had their work cut out for themselves, too.

Ponder it a little more. What would they eat? When they played instruments, what ethnic style dominated? When they danced, did they do the Hebrew Horah together? It would have been complicated. I am positive there was some reconciliation ministry that went on in this leadership summit. What was the unifying factor?

Eight Unifying Factors

The Lord Himself was the unifying factor in the leadership meeting at Antioch. Those who choose a lifestyle of revelation will also find the Lord as their primary unifying agent. Follow with me on eight little points that turned potential chaos into a time of cooperation.

1. They celebrated their diversity in unity instead of conformity of uniformity.

2. They ministered to the Lord. This became the key unifying factor. Everything else fades in the background when we center on Him.

3. Opposites attracted (school of the Spirit and school of the Word) and a new birth occurred: The ATM came into being!

4. They emphasized fasting as a lifestyle, not just as an issue of crisis intervention. They knew that sacrifice releases power.

5. The Holy Spirit moved in their midst with liberty to such an extent that the Scriptures record no name tags put on the prophecies. Awesome!

6. The jealousy of God came in their midst and God told them to "set apart for Me Barnabas and Saul." They had their priorities straight and gave Him first place.

7. After fresh consecration to the Lord first, Barnabas and Saul then gave themselves to "the work to which I have called them." They got the horse before the cart, as it should be. It is not as much work when He is pulling the load.

8. Without competition, jealousy or strife, they laid hands on them with prayer and fasting and sent Barnabas and Saul on their missionary journey. After this point Saul was called Paul (see Acts 13:9) and they were referred to as the apostolic team.

That Is Worth Dying For!

That is the kind of Kingdom collaboration we need to see in the Body of the Messiah. It is interesting that, according to Acts 11:26, it was in Antioch that the disciples were first called Christians. Such unity and testimony are worth praying for, fighting for and living for. And even more importantly, worth dying for.

Authentic, apostolic Christianity is being birthed in the Church once again. A call is going out for Kingdom collaborators who will function fully in their giftings while working cooperatively in a place of honor with others for Jesus' sake. Will you answer the call?

⟩ P R A Y E R ⟨

Father, for Jesus Christ's sake, I ask that You would change the understanding and expression of Christianity across the earth in this generation. I want Jesus to receive the rewards of His suffering.

Forgive Your Church for our petty competition and help us see one another as You see us. Teach us that unity is the celebration of diversity under Your Lordship. Deliver us from our fears of one another and teach us new ways of relating to each other, in Jesus' name. I want to do my part in the Body of Christ. Empower me to honor those around me and collaborate with them to see Your Kingdom come on earth as it is in heaven. May we become such partners in love, preferring one another, that the world will look on us and say, "Now there's a real Christian!" I pray this for the honor and glory of Jesus' great name in the earth. Amen.

⧫ Embracing Your Calling—Day 16

1. From your understanding, what transpired according to Acts 13:1–3? Compare this to the eight unifying factors above.

2. What has been your best experience in the Church today of honoring one another? What does it look like and what are the results?

3. In your life and ministry, how do you wed the "school of the Spirit" and the "school of the Word"?

4. Ask the Lord what role you have in Kingdom collaboration. What steps can you take today to be a unifying factor in your network or circle of influence?

Unity in Diversity

*In those days there was no king in Israel; everyone
did what was right in his own eyes.*

JUDGES 21:25

As we see in the above verse from Judges, when there is no king or
government in place, people are separated from one another by
their own judgments of right and wrong. There are no guidelines
for godly living. During those days in Israel's history, God raised
up men and women from among the populace to serve as leaders, "judges," during times of chaos and unrest. It was during
those times that unlikely leaders such as Gideon and Deborah
came to the forefront to speak forth God's intent and bring His
order to a disorderly people. Likewise, in the days ahead, God
is going to use unlikely people in both prophetic and apostolic
roles to facilitate a movement in the Church that will usher in
a powerful move of His Spirit on the earth. Let His glory fall!

My friend Tommy Tenney has some timeless words of wisdom that pound into us like well-driven nails:

Nothing disheartens me more than the lack of unity and the prevalence of division in the church. It is enough to break my heart, and I am just a brother. It has already broken the Father's heart.

The "game" being played out in the world today has high stakes for the church—the lost souls of men and women—and our "Coach" is calling us to act together in unity to win those souls for Him. Only when we become "one" and act in unity as Jesus prayed will we prove to be unstoppable, unbeatable and relentless in bringing down the gates of hell.

It is time the one unanswered prayer of Jesus Christ—when He prayed that we become one—be answered by the church—God's Dream Team.[1]

We saw in the previous day's reading that the prophetic and governmental roles, although they are quite different, complement each other. The prophetic role is to *hear* the instruction of God, and the governmental role is to *implement* that instruction. These roles represent a variety of gifts and ministry operations. Like facets of a diamond, they are different sides of the same sparkling gem. Building on this wisdom, let's see how the prophetic and the governmental can unite in their diversity to become "God's Dream Team."

Unity and Progress

Neither unity nor progress can be achieved without the true knowledge of God's will. If some puffed-up, fantasy-type word comes forth and we run with it, we may end up in shipwreck because such a word cannot produce God's will. Without true knowledge of His will clearly in place, we cannot become unified, nor will we make any noticeable progress.

Let's look at some Scriptures to see how this principle operates.

In the second year of Darius the king, on the first day of the sixth month, the word of the LORD came by the prophet Haggai to Zerubbabel the son of Shealtiel, governor of Judah, and to Joshua the son of Jehozadak, the high priest, saying. . . .

Haggai 1:1

Notice the action between the prophetic and the governmental in this passage. It is an Old Testament example of team ministry cooperation among the three offices of prophet (Haggai), priest (Joshua) and king (Zerubbabel).

Haggai released a word from God admonishing them to look at the condition of His "house," which lay "desolate" (verse 4). The people had said, "The time has not come, even the time for the house of the Lord to be rebuilt" (verse 2). But God said it was time to rise up, even when they did not think it was the right time. The *true* will of the Lord came forth to dispel the *perceived* will of God in their minds. And when the true word came, it released an appropriate action:

So the LORD stirred up the spirit of Zerubbabel the son of Shealtiel, governor of Judah, and the spirit of Joshua the son of Jehozadak, the high priest, and the spirit of all the remnant of the people; and they came and worked on the house of the LORD of hosts, their God.

verse 14

Note that the prophetically gifted must be sensitive to leaders and the problems they face within their bodies of believers. Prophetic words must come forth in a way that will encourage groups and congregations to heed the will of God and make changes, if needed. Prophetic types must not just run off and leave the leaders without making sure that the word was presented with grace and humility, and that it was received in the same way. Honor and accountability are important.

In this word from Haggai, true correction came forth, but also instruction that encouraged the people to change their previous mind-set and take hold of the vision to build. Every person, from the governor and high priest right on down to the remnant of the people, was stirred up and encouraged. Everyone took hold of the vision, because life was prophesied, not just the knowledge of their error. Then everyone came together in unity and made progress.

A real prophetic word has the potential for releasing an impartation of encouragement to motivate people to life. This is the goal of those who choose a lifestyle of revelation.

Unity Outside God's Will

It is possible for unity to occur *outside* the will of God even when the true will of God has come forth—and this is not good. First Kings 22 is a complicated chapter that I do not completely understand, but I want to share some things in it that warrant our attention.

The kings of Judah and Israel came together in unity to seek the Lord about making war on Syria to take back the territory of Ramoth-gilead. But King Jehoshaphat wanted the king of Israel to "inquire first for the word of the LORD" (verse 5). So the king of Israel gathered up four hundred prophets (that is a bunch of prophets!)—and guess what? They all agreed that Israel and Judah should go up to battle for the Lord "will give it into the hand of the king."

But Jehoshaphat was not sure about this word. Maybe he thought all these four hundred prophets were simply "yes men" to the king of Israel. He asked if there was another prophet available.

Let me insert here a recommendation to pastoral and apostolic leaders: Do not be intimidated by the prophetic. If a particular prophetic word does not sit just right with you, pay attention. It is always good to check things out with God. A word of instruction or admonition must ring true with you for you to implement the word successfully for the people. Unity can be made outside the will of God, but it will not result in the right kind of progress. Sometimes we think we know what the will of God is, but zeal without wisdom can cause us to proceed in the wrong direction.

So King Jehoshaphat sought more confirmation from God about the agreement to go to war. The king of Israel called on Micaiah—the prophet who usually said things the king of Israel did not like. At first Micaiah confirmed the other prophetic words. Perhaps he was tired of being the only one who put out disagreeable words and decided to go along with the crowd. But the king of Israel said to Micaiah, "How many times must I adjure you to speak to me nothing but the truth in the name of the LORD?" (verse 16). The governmental brought correction to the prophetic, and the prophetic then spoke the true word of the Lord. The true word that Micaiah brought was a corrective toward the governmental leaders—a serious word of warning.

In this story we see the possibilities for deception in the prophetic, even when there appears to be agreement. These kings had many issues of the heart that needed correction. It took the prophetic working in cooperation with governmental overseers to search out and find the true word of the Lord. The same is true for us today.

Tools for Unity in Diversity

No one office alone can properly build the Church. There is more than one tool in a toolbox. The most important is the one needed at the time. Let's look at five tools that will lead toward godly unity in our diversity.

Understanding

Each gifted person must seek to understand the other. The requirements of building the Church and the Kingdom include knowing when to call in what parts of the team to assist. This takes humility, availability, understanding and cooperation. To dishonor another servant or position or gifting of God is to dishonor God Himself. To have a viable revolution, we must restore the honor code.

I had the opportunity to be part of launching a national youth prayer movement initially called The Cause, joining Cindy Jacobs, Lou Engle, Chuck Pierce, Dutch Sheets and others to form the adult prophetic advisory council to this thrust. A wonderful young man from Connecticut named Billy Ostan was chosen to become the temporary national director. At the United States Strategic Prayer Conference held in Boston in November 2000, we laid hands on Billy and set him apart "to the Lord and for the work for which God has chosen him."

The first thing this young man did was call his parents to the platform, kneel before them and ask them to forgive him for any rebellion, whether in his heart or by his actions. The place was a puddle of water as we all wept before the Lord. He then stated publicly to them that he wanted to honor them in all that he did. What an example!

This kind of character is what is needed to unite the generations. Honor must flow both directions.

Honoring Authority

One of the keys to being in concert together is the art of honoring authority. Cindy Jacobs, co-founder of Generals of Intercession, addresses this needed area of spiritual protocol:

> One little-understood concept in the church today is that of honoring those in authority over us. This is probably because a

lack of respect for authority is becoming rampant in the youth of many cultures. . . . Of course, we are not to venerate leaders over us, but we do need to understand how to esteem and respect them. We honor them not just as people, but also for the positions in which the Lord has put them.[2]

Accountability

All governmental and prophetic vessels should be accountable to some kind of spiritual oversight, such as a denomination, fellowship, person, council, network of churches or ministry. Even if you are in itinerant ministry, you need to be part of a functioning local church. Maybe you are a mature, seasoned prophetic veteran and feel called to live in a quiet, secluded place to be able to hear the voice of God more readily. You, too, need to be accountable to and work in cooperation with other leaders in the Body of Christ. Every person at every level of ministry needs community and friendship. We all need counsel and confirmation to operate in the fullness of the gifts God has placed within us. Our health and safety are at stake. Take heed to the plan of God and become accountable to a proven group of leaders.

Dialogue

The goal is to have regular dialogue between prophetic and governmental ministries to facilitate cooperation. Communication is the key to understanding.

Some time ago the Lord gave me this wisdom word concerning the importance of communication: "The lack of communication breeds misunderstanding. Misunderstanding brings accusation. And accusation always results in some form of alienation."

Most divisions in the Church are not doctrinal in their foundation. Most deal with personal wounds. A personal hurt may have occurred and was never communicated through dialogue.

Most divorces are not the result of people disliking each other; they come from wounding and then failing to pursue accurate dialogue about the hurt. We must experience the sacrifice of communication. Dialogue and communication are the keys to walking together, learning together and building together.

Planning and Spontaneity

In the wedding of the prophetic and the governmental, we must learn to love both these qualities. Pastors and apostolic leaders must learn to appreciate the spontaneous combustion activity in which the prophetic operates so freely. Prophetic people must also embrace the importance of the steady planning methodology that many left-brained administrative people walk in. These elements together will bring balance to the Church and cause her to rise up as a glorious, healthy Bride.

Closing the Gender Gap

If we are to talk realistically about restoring authentic apostolic team ministry—my dream of ATM!—then sooner or later we must deal with the issue of women in ministry.

Women have been and are in ministry. That actually is not the issue. The issue is women in leadership. It is my firm conviction that great harm has been done to the Kingdom purposes of God because we have shot ourselves in our better foot. Believers are limping around in part because of the second-class status we men have relegated to many women.

Dr. Fuchsia Pickett, noted preacher, teacher and author, says it this way:

> It is difficult to estimate the damage that has been done to the Body of Christ because of prejudice against gender. What giftings, ministries, consolations, and virtues have been inadvertently

robbed from the Church because of strong prejudicial discrimi-
nation against the female gender! And what overt harm has been
perpetrated on the Church because of women's harsh reactions
against the limitations placed upon them that frustrated their
expression of the giftings of God in their lives.[3]

In the early days of Pentecostalism, the primary issue was
not sex but anointing. Edith Blumhofer, in *Pentecostal Women
in Ministry*, observes that "having the 'anointing' was far more
important than one's sex. As evangelistic bands carried the
full gospel across the country, women who were recognized
as having the anointing of the Holy Spirit shared with men
in preaching ministry. . . . A person's call—and how other believers viewed it—was far more important than [ministerial
credentials]."[4]

What am I getting at? When we talk about apostolic teams
emerging, let's remember the word *teams*. Teams have many
players functioning in many roles. We need secure leaders who
will graciously extend a biblical invitation to the women of our
land to come alongside them and walk in wonderful prophetic
anointing.

Prophetic Women in the Bible

Throughout biblical history, women have held key prophetic
roles and performed other important duties in God's army. Let's
look at the impact women have had in the places of service God
has entrusted to them.

Miriam (see Exodus 15:20). Miriam, the prophetess, stood
alongside Moses and Aaron as one of the three main leaders of
the Israelite nation as they left Egypt.

Deborah (see Judges 4:4). Deborah stood as judge before God
on behalf of Israel during this time, and she came alongside
Barak, a military authority, to lead the Israelite army to victory
against the Canaanites.

Huldah (see 2 Kings 22:14). Huldah was visited by the high priest, the scribe and a servant of the king so they could obtain the word of the Lord on behalf of young King Josiah. She must have been held in great regard by all of them.

Isaiah's wife (see Isaiah 8:3). We are not given her name, but the wife of Isaiah was a prophetess. What a team they must have made!

Elizabeth and Mary (see Luke 1:41–42, 46–47). This interchange recorded in Luke between Elizabeth, the mother of John the Baptist, and Mary, the mother of Jesus, resulted in exuberant praise and prophesying concerning the destiny of Mary's Child within.

Anna (see Luke 2:36–38). Anna was the praying prophetess present with Simeon the seer at the dedication of Jesus by His parents on His eighth day of life. A woman, a man; a prophetess, a seer: equal distribution with unique expressions of the same prophetic presence. As it was at the first coming of Jesus, so it will be at the Second Coming.

Philip's daughters (Acts 21:8–9). Philip the evangelist had four daughters who prophesied. Four in one family!

Other Women Leaders in the Bible

Jael (see Judges 4). She drove a tent peg into Sisera's head and delivered him into the hands of Barak. (Deborah had prophesied that the Lord would give Sisera to Barak. God did it through the hands of a woman.)

Abigail (see 1 Samuel 25). As an advocate, she pleaded the case of mercy to David (on the run from King Saul) on behalf of her wicked husband.

Esther. She was the godly queen who saved the Jewish race through her intercession.

Proverbs 31 woman. She was skillful in household and business issues, bought and sold real estate, ministered to the poor and more.

Woman at the well (see John 4). She is considered by many the first evangelist in the Bible, as she went forth proclaiming the Good News of the Christ.

Mary Magdalene (see Matthew 28:1–10). She was one of the women who were first at the tomb, first to hear that "He is risen" and first to announce His resurrection.

Lydia (see Acts 16:14–15). She is noted as the first convert in all of Europe.

Priscilla and Aquila (see Romans 16:3–5). They were probably a husband and wife teaching team explaining the Word of God with accuracy.

Phoebe (see Romans 16:1). She was a deaconess who washed the feet of the saints.

You can see through these many examples—if you needed any persuading—that women have always been used by God to do exploits in His Kingdom work on the earth. Women carry the gifting of the prophetic with sincerity and excellence equal to that of men. We need women in the prophetic ministry, as well in as other areas of gifting, to bring balance and strength to the coming prophetic revolution.

Women of the Church, you have been shackled long enough! As a man in the Church, I want to confess to you that we, the men of the Body of Christ, have feared you and have clung tightly to our rights, our positions, and our functions out of the fear that we would lose them to you. In our own insecurity and sin we have been unwilling to fully recognize your gifts, calling, and anointing in the Spirit or to accept you as full equals in the life and ministry of the Church. This might sound a bit brash, but in my opinion it is time for the "good old boys' club" to come to an end!

Therefore, I ask you, the women, to forgive us for holding you back, for not being cheerleaders for you, for not helping to equip you, and for not releasing you to fulfill God's calling on your lives. Forgive us for paying only lip service to your value, your gifts, your call, and your anointing. Forgive us for treating you like second-class citizens of the Kingdom and for not recognizing your equal status with us.[5]

Let's Do It Together

We are coming to a time when we more clearly appreciate and understand the various ministries of Christ. Let none of us deceive ourselves into believing that understanding in itself is equal to achievement. Understanding must motivate us to humility and prayer for God to establish mature, functioning role models among us.

Let's be grateful for each other. We need each other. Let's learn to defer to the gifts and ministries needed and approved for active service in the appropriate time. Let's seek and pray for divine cooperation so that a clear, rather than discordant, sound will be produced. Let's receive and honor the giftings of His most precious Holy Spirit in and through each other, so that the Church will be victorious and Jesus will be glorified. Let's do it together!

⟩ PRAYER ⟨

Father, I thank You for the glorious, many-faceted manifestations of Your Holy Spirit. Thank You for the unique gifts You have placed within each member of the Body of Christ. I celebrate the diversity of many members of the Body under the singular authority of our Head, Christ Jesus. What a wonder it is, Lord!

Now, Father, I ask that You come and grace us with the understanding of cooperation that will move us into immediate action and cause us to advance with new strength and vitality. Take the blinders off our eyes and the plugs out of our ears, and soften our hearts so that we can see, hear and receive each other in the true spirit of unity. Heal us where we have been wounded, restore our confidence in Your graces. Make me a unifying force in Your Body and help us create a symphony that will resound to the testimony of Jesus! Amen.

Embracing Your Calling—Day 17

1. Think of someone you have to work with who is very different from you—possibly someone with whom you have had a history of conflict. Ask the Lord to show you that person's heart and strengths, and how you can unite. What do you see? How do you see yourself working together more effectively for the Kingdom's sake?

2. What has been your approach to unity in the past? How has today's reading challenged you to think differently?

3. How can the apostolic and pastoral benefit from the prophetic? How can the prophetic benefit from apostolic and pastoral input?

4. Review the Tools for Unity in Diversity. Which tool will you make an effort to use today? How? Be specific.

Seizing Your Prophetic Destiny

God has a dream in His heart—and our God is a *big* dreamer. His vision is large enough to encompass a universe. He wants to instill this infinite dream in the hearts and minds of every believer, every family and every congregation in every city of every nation. But how can we, finite as we are, fulfill such a dream?

It takes a "corporate" heart to hold a vision from the God of this universe! It takes every believer working together in unified precision to grasp the totality of the dream proceeding from the heart of God. It takes a person intentionally living a lifestyle of intimacy, wisdom and revelation. And the only way we can be formed together as one is to catch the vision God has for our individual lives.

Our individual prophetic destiny is to catch and hold and live the unique life God has prepared for us as we dare to enter into His incredibly big dream. Only He knows how to blend millions of separate and diverse people into a unified and glorious Bride for the Son of His love. Each person, family, congregation, city and nation daring to seek and search out its individual destiny within the heart of God will become a flourishing member in the beloved Body of the glorified Church.

So while we hold on to our desire to share a corporate heart with other believers, let's dare to reach for our individual prophetic destiny. Let's seek and stretch and dare to dream big with our big God. His plan for you is unique and specially tailored to fit your individual destiny.

God's Plan for You

Let's start our quest for our prophetic destiny by reviewing what God's individually tailored plan for each of us involves.

Vision. "Where there is no vision, the people are unrestrained, but happy is he who keeps the law" (Proverbs 29:18). In this Scripture we see that without vision there is no restraint, no personal direction, just aimless, wandering people. Conversely, where there is vision, people are channeled in a specific direction. The result: happy people! We will talk more about the connection between restraint and vision in a moment.

Knowledge of God's law. "My people are destroyed for lack of knowledge. Because you have rejected knowledge, I also will reject you from being My priest. Since you have forgotten the law of your God, I also will forget your children" (Hosea 4:6). God was saying that the people had no revelatory knowledge because they had rejected His standards, and that darkness would pass down to the next generation.

Knowledge of His will. Paul prayed these following words apostolically as a father for the church of Colossae, and we can do the same, taking this Scripture and many others and turning them into devotional prayers for our lives and the lives of our families, congregations, cities and nations. Power resides in these words!

> For this reason also, since the day we heard of it, we have not ceased to pray for you and to ask that you may be filled with the knowledge of His will in all spiritual wisdom and understanding,

so that you will walk in a manner worthy of the Lord, to please Him in all respects, bearing fruit in every good work and increasing in the knowledge of God; strengthened with all power, according to His glorious might, for the attaining of all steadfastness and patience; joyously giving thanks to the Father, who has qualified us to share in the inheritance of the saints in Light.

Colossians 1:9–12

Once when I was away on one of my many travels, my late wife was crying out to the Lord out of sheer exhaustion. She was just plain weary, and she called out to Him for strength. Then she had a dream. When she awoke she could not remember what it was, but she knew it was significant. She looked at the clock; it read 1:11 A.M. She knew the Lord was trying to say something to her, so she searched out Psalm 1:11 and Proverbs 1:11 trying to find a Scripture that might be meaningful, but nothing connected. So she went back to sleep.

Then, in another dream, the Lord came to her. She saw Mike Bickle (senior pastor at the time and now the director of the International House of Prayer in Kansas City) with his Bible open, and he said, "It's Colossians 1:11."

She awoke from this dream and opened her Amplified Bible to Colossians 1:11: "[Be] invigorated and strengthened with all power, according to the might of His glory." Then the presence of the strength of God started coming on her with waves of strength and invigoration, and she knew God had answered her cry with "His glorious might." Glory to God!

Wisdom and revelation. I have prayed these following verses more often than any other set of verses I know. For about a ten-year period in my life, I prayed them almost daily, and then at least weekly for another decade–plus.

[I] do not cease giving thanks for you, while making mention of you in my prayers; that the God of our Lord Jesus Christ,

212

the Father of glory, may give to you a spirit of wisdom and of revelation in the knowledge of Him. I pray that the eyes of your heart may be enlightened, so that you will know what is the hope of His calling, what are the riches of the glory of His inheritance in the saints, and what is the surpassing greatness of His power toward us who believe.

Ephesians 1:16–19

Paul prayed this for the church of Ephesus, which at that time was viewed as the model church. But Paul saw they needed their hearts opened up so they could have three important things: *The knowledge of the hope of God's calling in their lives; revelatory understanding of the glorious inheritance that is in the saints;* and *revelatory understanding of the surpassing greatness of His power toward those who believe.* If the church at Ephesus needed these things, surely we need to have our eyes filled with light so that we can have them, too.

I ask the Father to open the shutter of the camera lens of my heart so it will be flooded with shafts of revelatory light. How does vision happen? Just as light enters a camera, vision comes through the lenses of our hearts. A picture is taken and the vision of God's plan for our destinies begins to unfold within our spirits. May His light bring you vision and revelation!

Future and hope. We are a chosen people, and God has chosen plans, purposes, destinies and pursuits for each of us. The following passage is a promise given to Jeremiah and a city and a whole generation. It is with us today as it was with them. God also wants to give us a future filled with hope.

"'I know the plans that I have for you,' declares the LORD, 'plans for welfare and not for calamity to give you a future and a hope. Then you will call upon Me and come and pray to Me, and I will

213

listen to you. You will seek Me and find Me when you search
for Me with all your heart.'"

Jeremiah 29:11–13

The word *vision* can be translated "revelation, mental sight or
a revealed word from God." Without a revealed word the people
will be unrestrained. This indicates the absence of guidance or
direction. But we are not to be aimless and without direction. A
restraint is like a bit in a horse's mouth. The bit is used not to
bind the horse but to give it direction. If you have no vision—a
revelation of God's destiny for your life—you will be without
direction, with no sense of His guidance. You will be perishing!
If you have vision, on the other hand, He will guide you into
your purpose, direction and destiny.

An anonymous writer penned these thoughts about the necessity of having a vision:

> A vision without a task is a dream.
> A task without a vision is drudgery.
> A vision with a task is the hope of the world.

Ten "Ds" to Help Us Dream

Can prophetically oriented people be of any earthly good? Absolutely! But while many people, leaders, congregations and cities
aim at nothing and hit it, we must be a people who dare to dream
God's dreams. God wants us to delight in Him, and He will put
His desires, dreams and determinations for destiny within us.

The following words of guidance are inspired (although not
directly quoted) from my friend William Greenman of Purpose
International, gleaned from his first book, *How to Find Your
Purpose in Life*.[1]

1. *Delight*. "Delight yourself in the Lord" (Psalm 37:4).
   Opening your heart and soul to receive the knowledge of

God's will is a prerequisite. There is nothing better than His will. It is wonderful, majestic, powerful. And as we delight in Him, something transpires: He changes us.

2. *Desire.* "He will give you the desires of your heart" (Psalm 37:4). *Desire* means "to long for, crave, yearn or covet." We are to be passionate people motivated to pursue God's purposes for our generation. As we make Him our delight, He puts His passionate yearnings in our heart, "for it is God who is at work in you, both to will and to work for His good pleasure" (Philippians 2:13). God gives us the will, the desire and the ability to perform His good pleasure. The key here is *delight.*

One of the things I absolutely cannot stand is passion-less Christianity! You can call it religion, but do not call it Christianity. If we want to be people who seize our prophetic destiny, we must become passion-filled—people on fire, hot with the love of God.

3. *Dream.* "Where there is no vision, the people are unrestrained" (Proverbs 29:18). People who have no dream are without direction. Webster's dictionary says that a dream is "a fond hope or a vision." Let's be people willing to dream.

4. *Destiny.* Your dream will guide you into your destiny. Webster's defines *destiny* as "an inevitable series of events or that which determines those events, that is a supernatural thing." We must plan a dream to turn it into a destiny.

5. *Decision.* Deuteronomy 30:19 explains that God has given us the choice of "life and death, the blessing and the curse." When you choose to follow the dream that the Lord places in your heart, you are choosing life. When you make this quality decision of the heart, you start the sanctification process. This is part of delighting in Him and doing what delights Him, and it moves you out of self-motivation and selfish ambition. He will sanctify you (set you apart) as you choose His will and move toward it.

6. *Determination.* Once having decided to run with the vision that God has placed in your heart, you will then be forced to exercise determination. Resolve that nothing will stop you. "Run with endurance the race that is set before [you]" (Hebrews 12:1). It does not mean the road is without obstacles. In fact, the forces of hell and darkness will try to hinder and defeat you. But you must keep running and not look back.

7. *Dedication.* After you have determined in your heart that you will act on the vision God has given you, you must dedicate yourself to it. As you devote yourself to the vision, you are giving yourself to the Lord. Your dedication will be received by Him as an act of worship.

8. *Discipline.* "Discipline yourself for the purpose of godliness" (1 Timothy 4:7). Once you have dedicated yourself, you must exercise discipline. It takes discipline—the training that develops self-control, character, orderliness and efficiency—to devote yourself to your dream. Do not throw out spiritual disciplines, thinking they are too "religious." We do not discipline ourselves to earn points with God. That is performance-based acceptance. But we need to pray, read the Word, fast and be part of a committed people who will walk together toward the dreams God has placed in our hearts. Sometimes it may feel dry, boring and uneventful, but keep pressing on. This discipline will bring character formation to make you a vessel that can carry the glory of the Lord. (Read Matthew 25:23 and Luke 19:17 on the related subject of faithfulness.)

9. *Death.* "Truly, truly, I say to you, unless a grain of wheat falls into the earth and dies, it remains alone; but if it dies, it bears much fruit" (John 12:24). At some point the Lord may ask you to give back to Him the vision you have received from Him. It is like Abraham giving up Isaac. It hurts like everything, and you wonder what in the world

is going on. But God's purpose is to see how sticky and gooey possessive you have become, and to make sure you know the vision is His.

10. *Diligence.* "A righteous man falls seven times, and rises again" (Proverbs 24:16). That is diligence! Do not quit. Quitters never win and winners never quit. *Diligence* means "to be constant, to make careful and continual effort." Romans 12:11 encourages us not to "[lag] behind in diligence" but to be "fervent in spirit, serving the Lord."

Once I had a dream in which I was being introduced from a new platform, in a conference setting, by Dr. Don Finto of Nashville, whom I consider an apostolic father. In the dream the people I was addressing were a little antsy. Things did not seem to be going well. So I got up to speak and said, "I want to teach you about times of transition." All ears perked up then. And even though I was asleep, I, too, became attentive and perked up my own spiritual ears so I could hear what I was about to say!

In the dream I said, "There are three points you must always remember when going through a time of transition. First, you must always remember that it is God who is at work in your life, to will and to work for His good pleasure. Second, you must trust God's word that has been given to you, because it will not return void, but will accomplish the very purpose for which He sent it. And third, always remember that God wants you to do His will more than you want to. God will help you do it."

What an unusual dream—one filled with wonderful guidance from the Lord!

The Goal Is God Himself!

Kenneth W. Osbeck reminds us of the two shoe salesmen sent to a primitive island. The first salesman wired back, "Coming home immediately. No one here wears shoes." The second man wired, "Send a boatload of shoes immediately. The possibilities for selling shoes here are unlimited." Comments Osbeck, "May we as believers be characterized as people of vision—'looking unto Jesus, the author and finisher of our faith.' (Hebrews 12:2)."[2]

Ultimately it is not the vision, plan or purpose that is God's goal. *His goal is to be your delight.* When we put the cart before the horse, we give God's vision and purpose precedence over God Himself. We can become driven people who use God, instead of people who serve God. When this happens, God must oppose us and turn us around so we can be formed into the image of His Son. Jesus was never driven to fulfill a ministry or vision; He was compelled by love to do the will of the Father, whatever the cost. He was not purpose-driven but Person-driven.

Paul shared the same goal: "Forgetting what lies behind and reaching forward to what lies ahead, I press on toward the goal for the prize of the upward call of God in Christ Jesus" (Philippians 3:13–14). The upward call is not becoming a pastor or prophet or having a great healing ministry. The upward call is being conformed into the image of Jesus Christ.

As we conclude this day's reading, read or sing with me the lyrics of the eighth-century Irish hymn "Be Thou My Vision":

> Be thou my Vision, O Lord of my heart;
> Naught be all else to me, save that thou art;
> Thou my best thought, by day or by night,
> Waking or sleeping, thy presence my light.
>
> Be thou my Wisdom, and thou my true Word;
> I ever with thee and thou with me, Lord;
> Thou my great Father, and I thy true son,
> Thou in me dwelling, and I with thee one.
>
> Riches I heed not, nor man's empty praise;
> Thou mine inheritance, now and always;

Thou and thou only, first in my heart,
High King of heaven, my treasure thou art.

Be thou my breast-plate, my sword for the fight;
Be thou my armour, and be thou my might;
Thou my soul's shelter, and thou my high tower;
Raise thou me heavenward, O Power of my power.

High King of heaven, my victory won,
May I reach heaven's joys, O bright heaven's Sun!
Heart of my own heart, whatever befall,
Still be my Vision, O Ruler of all.

I can tell you from experience that, at times, you must let the vision die so the Lord can help you die to self. This is the pattern of life that leads to multiplication. God is well able to resurrect any dream or vision He chooses. You might have heard of the lost ax head that floated on water! (See 2 Kings 6:5–7.) He will release grace to help us do what He desires most—become lovers of God and people of character and carriers of His glory.

⊣ PRAYER ⊢

Holy Father, I want to be a lover of God, a person of character, a carrier of Your glory. I am continually amazed at the grace and mercy You pour out on me as I stumble along the path of life. You have designed an incredible plan for me, and I desire with all my heart to live the life that Jesus died to give me, and to walk securely on the paths You have designed for me.

Father, I ask for the power of Your Holy Spirit to come and assist me in this quest for my prophetic destiny. Speak again to my heart the desire You have for me, and change my selfish desires into Your own perfect will. I ask for dreams, visions, words of knowledge and prophetic utterances to

*come forth and point the way toward Your purposes. The
dreams You have given me that have been lost or forgotten
or trampled on, I ask that by Your redemptive grace You
come and restore them to me again.*

*Come, Lord, and be my vision. Walk beside me as I seize
my prophetic destiny. Help me know You more intimately
and be changed into the likeness of Your dear Son and my
dear Savior. Amen.*

Embracing Your Calling—Day 18

1. Has God given you a vision? Describe it or what has been
   revealed to you so far. Remind yourself the words of the
   apostle Paul: to forget what lies behind, reach forward
   to what lies ahead, and "press on toward the goal for the
   prize of the upward call of God in Christ Jesus" (Philippians 3:13–14).

2. Which two Ds of the "Ten 'Ds' to Help Us Dream" above
   do you perceive the Lord wants you to focus on at this
   time? Why? What are some practical steps you can take
   to seize your prophetic destiny?

3. Which do you feel you have pursued most passionately:
   your purpose or the Person of Jesus Christ? Why? Remind
   yourself that the upward call is being conformed into the
   image of Jesus Christ.

4. Take time right now to pray Colossians 1:9–12 or Ephesians 1:10–19. May your eyes be filled with His revelatory
   light to perceive and seize your prophetic destiny.

Growing in Revelation

On two different occasions Jesus told His disciples that to those who have, "more shall be given, and he will have an abundance" (Matthew 13:12; 25:29). On the first occasion he was speaking of knowing the mysteries of the Kingdom of heaven; on the second He was speaking of being responsible with the resources God provides. What an amazing promise: to those who have, more will be given. And not just a little; you will have abundance!

In both situations Jesus followed these words with a sobering warning: "[B]ut whoever does not have, even what he has shall be taken away from him." This is why walking in the prophetic is designed to be a lifestyle and not just something you do when you feel like it. Jesus wants you to continue to grow and not become stagnant or fall away.

Growing in the Prophetic Grace

Let's look at some principles that will help you continue to grow in a prophetic lifestyle. These also can apply to families, congregations, denominations, cities and nations. God desires that everyone comes to the knowledge of the truth (see 1 Timothy 2:4).

Research Your Foundations

Asking great questions leads to finding great answers. Many questions need to be asked: What is your family's history, ethnic background, religious heritage and so on? Who were the founders of your city, nation or church? What were their goals, visions, purposes and origins?

What does your name mean? Is there a promise contained within it? What is the name of your city, church or denomination? Whom are you named after? What is the outstanding characteristic of your namesake? Redemptively, turn names into promises as a tool of discovering your prophetic destiny. Claim your generational inheritance and call forth the blessing. Remember, the power of the blessing is greater than the power of the curse.

Researching your foundations can help you know how to build properly and what potential opportunities may exist for personal growth and development. Study to show yourself approved.[1]

Pick Up the Baton

Not all promises have to be received directly by you or by your generation. Receive the inheritance of those who have gone before. Daniel 9:2 shows an example of receiving the baton of promise of a previous generation, the promise given in Jeremiah 29:10: "When seventy years have been completed for Babylon, I will visit you and fulfill My good word to you, to bring you back to this place." What are the unfulfilled promises that have gone before you? Research them, pick them up and seize them for your life and generation.

Gain Insight from Others

Particular gifts of the Spirit such as the discerning of spirits, the word of knowledge and the gift of prophecy are valuable here. They will assist you in determining specific points the Lord wants you to know as you seek to grow in revelation. Reach out to trusted intercessors and find out what they are discerning. What are the current-day revelatory promises? What are trusted prophetic voices saying? What is the voice of the Holy Spirit saying to you personally?[2]

Walk in Unity and Accountability

Each person needs to walk in a committed relationship with a local expression of the Body of Christ. They will greatly assist you as you grow in your specific destiny. What are your authorities saying? Are you walking in unity and counsel with others? We must each find confirmation, wisdom and counsel through the safety net of walking circumspectly with others.

Kneel on the Promises

Now let's take those confirmed, authentic promises and remind God of His Word:

> On your walls, O Jerusalem, I have appointed watchmen; all day and all night they will never keep silent. You who remind the LORD, take no rest for yourselves; and give Him no rest until He establishes and makes Jerusalem a praise in the earth.
>
> Isaiah 62:6–7

Pray those precious promises into being. Humbly yet boldly lay hold of God, and do not let Him go until you see His Kingdom come, His will done on earth (and in your life) as it is in heaven. Follow the examples of the revivalist of old, but do not just stand on the promises—kneel on them! Give birth to them, for Jesus' sake.

Proclaim the Promises

We are not called just to discern the darkness; we are called to turn on the light. One of the powerful ways of doing this is through the power of proclamation. We can join praise with prayer and pronounce "to the rulers and the authorities in the heavenly places" (Ephesians 3:10) that the power of the blessing is greater than the power of the curse. By announcing God's Word, we release individual and corporate declarations of the will of God. Watch faith ignite and destinies unfold.[3]

Act in the Opposite Spirit

There is nothing that stops growth more quickly than the poison of bitterness, resentment and unforgiveness. When hurt or wronged in any way, forgive. Forgiveness is letting your desire for justice go because you trust the God of justice to make things right in His way and His time. One way to respond when this happens is to act in the opposite spirit. What does this mean? If you are cursed, bless. If you discern powers of greed and materialism, then look for opportunities to give and minister to the poor. If the enemy tempts you to hate, then sow deeds of love, forgiveness and kindness. Turn the tables on the enemy by doing the servant works of Christ.

Write It Down

Habakkuk 2:2 gives us the details and reason for these activities: "Record the vision and inscribe it on tablets, that the one who reads it may run." Writing down God's promise ensures that it will be kept before your eyes and properly passed on to the next generation.[4]

Step Out

Nothing takes the place of stepping out of your comfort zone and out onto the end of the limb. Remember that faith is always spelled r-i-s-k. We must formulate practical plans of implementation, wait on God, get His mind and timing on the matter—and then get up and go, obey and step out.

Some people need to hear words like *wait, listen, pray* and *slow down.* Others need words like *get up, get going, rise up* and *do something.* Eventually we must add works, or corresponding actions, to our faith (see James 2:14–26). So in order to grow and seize your prophetic destiny, step out. God is not only good, but He will catch you if you fall and help you get up and try again.

Pursue God

Growth takes time and patience. We are programmed in this culture of ours to expect instant results, so we must set our minds and hearts toward persistence and perseverance. Our prophetic destinies lie in knowing the God who designed them. Give yourself wholeheartedly to the pursuit of knowing Him in all His fullness; then He will surely reveal whom He has created you to be in the midst of your pursuit. Our goal is not the plan, but the Man, Christ Jesus.

Releasing the Gift of Prophecy

The early teachings that Jesus gave His disciples highlighted the rewards of giving.

> "Give, and it will be given to you. They will pour into your lap a good measure—pressed down, shaken together, and running over. For by your standard of measure it will be measured to you in return."
>
> Luke 6:38

Do you love that? As you give, God's blessings will be poured out (not sprinkled) in good measure (not just enough to get by)—pressed down, shaken together and running over! As you walk out a lifestyle of revelation, sharing what you have received is one sure way not just to grow in revelation, but also to receive more. Let's look at some practical principles for releasing this gift of the Holy Spirit.

Prophecies may be expressed or delivered:

1. By simply speaking them (see 1 Corinthians 14:4, 6, 19).

2. Through demonstrative actions (see 1 Samuel 15:26–28; Acts 21:10–11).

3. Through writing them down (see Jeremiah 36:4–8, 15–18; Revelation 1:11).

4. Through song or musical instrumentation (see 2 Kings 3:15; 1 Chronicles 25:1, 3; Ephesians 5:19; Colossians 3:16).

5. Through anointed intercession, privately or publicly (e.g., Daniel), or by praying a prophetic blessing releasing God's grace.

6. As a *rhema* word in the midst of preaching or sharing with others.

7. In the context of "the spirit of counsel" (Isaiah 11:2) without the endorsement of "thus saith the Lord."

8. By an individual, and then submitted to the local pastoral eldership team for judgment, appraisal, prayer and application. It then becomes their responsibility; the prophet's responsibility has been fulfilled.

9. Not right away. You do not have to release everything you receive. Wait for a confirmation of two or three witnesses. Put it into your spiritual filing cabinet (called "pending") and wait for the other pieces of the puzzle to appear before you speak.

10. Not at all! Some things are not to be shared. They are God's revelatory treasures just for you, as one friend speaking to another.

Each local leadership or apostolic/pastoral team is given the responsibility to determine the wisdom administration of the revelatory gifts. While these gifts are meant to be expressed not only within the Church but also in the marketplace, it is helpful to learn and grow in the context of a healthy, safe body of believers who know how to nurture the prophetic.

The goal of all of this is to grow in the revelatory grace on our lives. Pursue love, pursue the Lord and eagerly desire His wonderful gifts, especially that you may prophesy (see 1 Corinthians 14:1). This is how you will grow and how you will help the Body to grow as well.

When Prophecy Does Not Flow

So what should you do when the revelatory grace on your life does not seem to be flowing as it used to? Well, there is not one solution that fits all, but here are some principles to follow.

Scripture says that if you are faithful in a little, you will be given much. Do not despise small beginnings in operating in the gift of prophecy. If you are faithful to give the small word the Spirit gives, your capacity to receive more will increase, and the gift will begin to flow richly and freely.

If you or your church body seems to be stuck or has stopped flowing altogether, there may be some sin or error that has not been recognized and corrected. The Lord is quick to forgive and cleanse once repentance has been expressed, and you can ask Him to restore the gift and then believe for a renewal to occur and increase to come. Remember that you will mess up from time to time, but your Father desires to express His love to you through His kind discipline and correction. His mercies are new every morning! So be quick to forgive yourself, too, and move on in the flow of the Spirit. Dust yourself off and get going again.

The following is a list of some major reasons why the prophetic does not flow and ways to respond to correct the situation. Read this list prayerfully and ask the Lord to highlight anything that might apply to your experiences. Understanding these principles is absolutely essential for living a lifestyle of revelation. The light of God's truth brings healing and freedom and will keep you on His straight and narrow path.

1. *Ignorance.* "My people are destroyed for lack of knowledge" (Hosea 4:6). Due to insufficient teaching, areas of ministry may appear weak or undernourished. Your response: Instruction needs to be given; then faith and hunger will result.

2. *Fear.* "God has not given us a spirit of timidity, but of power and love and discipline" (2 Timothy 1:7). This could include:

   Fear of people, even leadership (rejection, being misunderstood).

   Fear of missing God and saying something wrong, or of saying something out of one's own mind.

   Fear that one's faith will fail in the middle of the delivery.

   Fear of embarrassment, failure.

   Your response: As the Lord told Joshua three times, "Be strong and courageous!" (Joshua 1:6–7, 9).

3. *Pushing prophesying out of reach.* By taking the attitude that prophecy is out of the reach of the ordinary believer, or by making the detailed word of knowledge of the prophetic the standard, we can intimidate others from sharing their "less impressive" gifting. Your response: Share whatever God has given to you regardless of how great or small you think it is.

4. *Closed environment.* By not staying exposed to an environment in which the prophetic is flowing, you miss out

228

on associational training. Your response: Find a healthy, prophetic culture to be a part of. If you drink from a river long enough, you, too, will take on its properties. Association and environment must be created and maintained for the revelatory presence to be sustained.

5. *Not living in the Word*. If the Word of Christ is not dwelling in a person richly, then the Spirit has little to draw from. The breath of God blows upon the written Word of God. Your response: Be more impressed by the Word going into you than the Word coming out of you.

6. *Inconsistent prayer*. It is by being in God's presence that we receive His word. We must be consistent in prayer. No prayer life, no revelatory life. Your response: Pray. Active prayer life, active revelatory life.

7. *Pride*. By wanting to start at the top, we circumvent the natural progression of growth. With a desire to be deep and profound rather than to stick with the simple, we stop up the prophetic flow. Motivation is the central issue. Your response: Humble yourself. The Lord honors humility. Be a servant and increase will come.

8. *Grieving the Holy Spirit*. Due to errors of the past (by an individual, a fellowship, even a denomination or region), the Holy Spirit may have been grieved. Your response: You must confess your ways and seek His restored prophetic life flow again. This may take months or even years, but eventually you will see new growth in burned fields. I have seen this pattern in many cities. As repentance is cultivated, old wells can and are often re-dug. Like Isaac, re-dig the ancient wells of His presence.

How to Grow in Genuine Prophetic Ministry

Following are three simple guidelines that will help you to grow in a lifestyle of revelation and genuine prophetic ministry.

Guideline #1: Test the Spirits

"Test the spirits to see whether they are from God" (1 John 4:1). What idea, concept, teaching or information is coming forth? What is the heart of the issue? Is Jesus presented as the Source of life? Is His cross lifted up?

Graham Cooke, author and prophetic minister, states, "Allowing prophecy without testing it . . . leads to abuse within the ministry, a discrediting of the gift in general, a poor model for local believers to follow, and frustration of the purpose for which true prophecy is given."[5]

Derek Prince wrote, "To permit the exercise of prophecy without requiring it to be subjected to scriptural judgment is against the teaching of the New Testament, and commonly leads to abuses which discredit prophecy as a whole and frustrate the purposes for which true prophecy is given."[6]

Guideline #2: Do Not Be a Prophecy Junkie!

The revelatory word complements and does not compete with the written Word of God. Be a "Wordaholic" first. Let the revelatory gifting be the dessert, not the main course. Store the Word of God in your heart and meditate on the written Word, giving the breath of God something to blow on to quicken as a spoken word in your life.

Guideline #3: Understand the Nature of the Prophetic

Knowledge is not our primary goal; prophetic revelations are signposts pointing the way to the One who is the answer. We want more than information; we want intimacy with God. Here are some related guidelines.

- Few words are declarations that something will automatically come into being. Most words are invitations to respond to God with conditions that must first be met.

- Few prophetic words are immediate, "now" words. Most help us in the process of growth and becoming.
- Few prophetic words get us out of a problem. They are used to shed light, comfort and encourage us to continue on. There are no shortcuts with God.
- Focus not on the promise but on the God who promised. Direct your faith onto the God of the Word. When our faith is misplaced, it produces fantasy and unreal expectations.
- Realize the "clarity and cost" equation. What God counts as significant will often arouse great opposition by the enemy. Paul was warned repeatedly of how much he would suffer for Christ's sake. Every promise contains a cost.
- Give room for "time lapse." As most words are invitations toward an end, expect a duration of time in between while the person is being prepared for the promise that is on the way.

Do Not Throw It Out!

As we grow to discern prophetic revelations and try to process them effectively, we may experience some frustration and confusion. At some point we may be tempted to throw the whole package of this gifting out the window. Do not do it! It takes time and patience to develop your spiritual antennae, and that is what this relationship with Jesus is all about—communicating. We must be committed to learning God's methods of communication.

Here are some helpful tactics to employ while you are in training. And in reality, we always remain in training as we go from glory to glory.

Do Not Put Out the Spirit's Fire

"Do not put out [despise, quench] the Spirit's fire [passion, zeal]; do not treat prophecies with contempt" (1 Thessalonians

5:19–20, NIV). Due to errors, failures and abuses, we may be tempted to despise the whole mess. But do not put out the Holy Spirit's fire by overreacting.

Do Not Be Quickly Shaken

"[Do not] be quickly shaken from your composure or be disturbed either by a spirit or a message or a letter as if from us, to the effect that the day of the Lord has come" (2 Thessalonians 2:2). Do not become easily unsettled or alarmed by some prophecy. And avoid two ditches: one, discarding and rejecting prophecy altogether; and, two, being enamored of and captivated by it.

Hold Fast to What Is Good

Moving in the prophetic is well worth the journey, even though there are valleys along the way. Great benefit will come as we cultivate the character we need to carry the revelatory gifts. "I, the prisoner of the Lord, implore you to walk in a manner worthy of the calling with which you have been called" (Ephesians 4:1). First Thessalonians 5:21 urges us to "examine everything carefully; hold fast to that which is good."

=====⟩ **P R A Y E R** ⟨=====

Father God, thank You for the revelatory grace on my life. What a wonderful gift! You are the gift. You have humbly and selflessly poured Yourself into my life. In the same way I desire to pour out my life as an offering, a pleasing offering to You. In any areas where I have stopped growing, I ask that You would initiate new growth again. Lord Jesus, I want to continue to grow in genuine prophetic ministry representing Your glorious image and the testimony of Jesus. Empower me to walk worthy of the calling with which I have been called. I choose to forget what lies behind, reaching forward to what lies ahead and pressing on toward the goal for the prize of the upward call of God in Christ Jesus. I am holding fast to what is good, Jesus—You! Amen.

Embracing Your Calling—Day 19

1. What has helped you to grow in the prophetic grace God has given to you?

2. What insight from today's reading do you want to implement to increase or accelerate your growth?

3. Have you experienced a shift or a stoppage in the prophetic flow in your life? What have you done to "unclog" and restore the flow?

4. Has frustration or confusion with the prophetic tempted you to "throw it out"? Take a moment to review the Scriptures in the "Do Not Throw It Out!" section above. Read them; meditate on them. Recommit yourself to the journey and lifestyle of revelation.

Prophesy Life!

In today's reading we are going to study a prophetic Scripture from the book of Ezekiel that demonstrates the title of this reading. We will look at Ezekiel 37 with a New Testament set of lenses. I want to crash, bam, break up and annihilate some wrong Old Testament concepts that some of us have in our minds concerning the way we see prophets today, the way we look at the things prophets do and the messes they can leave behind.

Our concepts must change if we are fully to seize our prophetic destinies in God. We cannot operate from outdated and wrong interpretations of Old Covenant concepts of prophetic people and revelation. We must see with New Covenant vision in order to operate effectively in the revolution that will bring global change to the Body of Christ.

Give your present mind-set to the Lord as we delve into this wonderful passage of God's Word.[1]

The Valley through a New Testament Lens

Let's look at the entire passage of Ezekiel 37:1–10. Then we will break it down and draw out some principles that may surprise you.

The hand of the LORD was upon me, and He brought me out by the Spirit of the LORD and set me down in the middle of the valley; and it was full of bones. He caused me to pass among them round about, and behold, there were very many on the surface of the valley; and lo, they were very dry. He said to me, "Son of man, can these bones live?" And I answered, "O Lord GOD, You know."

Again He said to me, "Prophesy over these bones and say to them, 'O dry bones, hear the word of the LORD.' Thus says the Lord GOD to these bones, 'Behold, I will cause breath to enter you that you may come to life. I will put sinews on you, make flesh grow back on you, cover you with skin and put breath in you that you may come alive; and you will know that I am the LORD.'"

So I prophesied as I was commanded; and as I prophesied, there was a noise, and behold, a rattling; and the bones came together, bone to its bone. And I looked, and behold, sinews were on them, and flesh grew and skin covered them; but there was no breath in them.

Then He said to me, "Prophesy to the breath, prophesy, son of man, and say to the breath, 'Thus says the Lord GOD, "Come from the four winds, O breath, and breathe on these slain, that they come to life."'" So I prophesied as He commanded me, and the breath came into them, and they came to life and stood on their feet, an exceedingly great army.

Ezekiel 37:1–10

We are going to look at these verses in Ezekiel 37 through lenses described by Paul in 1 Corinthians 14:3: "One who prophesies speaks to men for edification and exhortation and consolation." This is also the way we as Christians—who live with almighty God in the reality of the New Covenant—are to view the prophetic.

Yes, the office of the prophet does additionally move in the realms of declaring direction and correction, whereas the simple gift of prophecy does not include these dimensions. But for the time being let's view this passage with the redemptive perspective that even tearing down is ultimately for the purpose of building up.

The Temporary Condition: Are These Bones Dry!

Too many people have the idea that God has a clenched fist and is ready to hammer us with words of judgment every chance He gets. Thus they view the prophetic lifestyle as one in which God continually pours out His wrath toward a wayward people through whoever is unfortunate enough to receive and convey His vengeful words.

No, no, a thousand times, no! That is not the connotation of the word *hand of God* in this Scripture: "The hand of the LORD was upon me" (Ezekiel 37:1). The word for *hand* here, in Hebrew, is *yad*, which means "the open hand of God." It was the *open* hand of God that was on Ezekiel—open to release a blessing, to edify, exhort and console.

"And He brought me out by the Spirit of the LORD and set me down in the middle of the valley; and it was full of bones" (verse 1). Sometimes we get overspiritualized notions of what it means to be "in the Spirit." If we are going to be in the Spirit, we must be so heavenly minded that we are definitely going to do some earthly good. Here Ezekiel, led by God's Spirit, was given an "otherly" perspective so that he could release the life of the Spirit in practical ways.

"He caused me to pass among them round about, and behold, there were very many on the surface of the valley; and lo, they were very dry" (verse 2). Ezekiel here was making an observation about the condition of these bones: They were dry, fragmented and in great disarray. Many times we get words of knowledge about the present or even past conditions in a church, city, nation or an individual's life, and it might not look too great. It might look dark and even hopeless. But God does not intend to leave us in that condition. God desires to give us remedies for our illnesses and evils. He has a solution for all our pollution. He wants to give the Church a hope-filled word so we can move out of the dry places we find ourselves in. That is the purpose of prophetic revelation.

When I was a young pastor, a nationally recognized leader came to our city to minister. We held the meetings on the local university campus in hopes of making it more of an outreach. The noted guest speaker detected that our fellowship was experiencing a difficult and dry time. He spoke from what he saw at that time and not from our prophetic potential. Basically he told us to dig around for a year, see if there was any life and, if not, to write *Ichabod* over it and shut it down. His word was not encouraging at all. I made a determination through that painful process that if the Lord ever released me to go minister at other churches and cities, my goal would be to encourage them, not to deflate them.

God has a word of wisdom (prescription) to go along with every word of knowledge (diagnosis). Medical doctors follow up with a prescription after giving a diagnosis. Should we as followers of the Great Physician not do the same—or even better?

Next, God's question to Ezekiel was an invitation to intervention. "He said to me, 'Son of man, can these bones live?' And I answered, 'O Lord GOD, You know'" (verse 3).

Ezekiel responded honestly by admitting he did not know, but that he was sure God did. To Ezekiel they looked dry and lifeless, but maybe God had a different perspective. He was right, God did. And prophetic revelations are invitations from God to bring change to situations, circumstances and temporary problem areas of life. We are invited into divine cooperation. Remember, God knows the answer—but He has predetermined to involve us in bringing His solution.

God wants to bring us remedies and teach us how to declare life. Ezekiel did not know about those bones, but God was preparing to show him something awesome. The prophetic is an invitation to see the open hand of God release His blessing on hopeless, helpless lives.

Can the dry bones of your life, family or city live?

Prophesy over These Bones

Now we learn the purpose of the prophetic: "Again He said to me, 'Prophesy over these bones and say to them, "O dry bones, hear the word of the LORD"'" (Ezekiel 37:4).

The purpose of the prophetic is this: to speak the word of the Lord to dry bones. Leaders in the Church need to be speaking to the dry bones of the Body of Christ that they might rise up and live. Believers need to unite and declare life over the broken, fragmented structures of society. For Jesus' sake, let's transform the very darkest places into centers of revival and light.

"To prophesy" is simply to speak or sing, with inspiration, the current mind or heart of God. We are to release God's life by declaring life to dry people, dry places, dry churches and dry cities.

Have you noticed that in the New Testament we do not find prophetic words given with the verbiage of "Thus saith the Lord"? That is primarily an Old Testament model. I suggest that we need a more down-to-earth delivery to put the word of the Lord within reach of people. His message is coming not to make a grandiose display of flowery and exaggerated words, but to help people. Simple presentations delivered in a humble style can make a profound impact on another's life when it is the true word of the Lord.

At the London Prayer Summit in June 2000, I was speaking on the theme "Creating an Opening," but my attention kept being drawn toward a gentleman to my right. Every time I glanced his way, syllables kept running through my mind that sounded like *A-la-ha-bad*. It started becoming persistent, even a bit annoying.

I knew in my spirit it was the name of a city, but my mind kept attempting to analyze as I was preaching: *Now that's either in Pakistan or Afghanistan.* I would look at the hungry gentleman and strong impressions would come, yet my natural mind would argue, *Don't make a fool of yourself. You don't know what nation he's from, and you can't even say it right!* All the while I was preaching away on the necessity of being a people of God's presence.

Finally I grew just plain tired of the inner debate, walked over to him and in proper British English, not my Nashvillian slang, blurted, "Conrad of Allahabad."

I was not even sure what I had said.

His reaction was startling; his eyes opened really wide.

I proceeded to announce that he had come from India to London to catch the spirit of prayer, and that he would return to his city and begin a 24-hour house of prayer.

The man looked both shaken and enlightened. It was obvious that life had been imparted.

Later he said to me, "You told me my name and what city I was from. How did you know those things?"

I looked at him and said, "I didn't."

He reacted quickly. "Yes, you did! My name is Conrad and I'm from the city of Allahabad on the Ganges River in India, where every year thirty to forty million Hindus come to wash themselves of their sin. I came here to get an impartation for prayer since I want to start a house of prayer in one of India's darkest cities."

Praise the Lord! Life had been spoken. Vision had been imparted. The "hope lights" had come on, and Conrad returned home to Allahabad, India, filled with faith.

One of the amazing things to *me* was that I had spoken in British English with the correct vowel pronunciation and emphasis on the right syllables. For a guy who grew up in Cowgill, Missouri, a town of 259 people, that is a cultural miracle!

But the real point is, God wants us to look deeply into His heart and breathe forth His blessings into and over the broken circumstances we see around us in a way people are able to receive. Build a bridge to carry your cargo, not a wall they cannot see over.

> "Thus says the Lord GOD to these bones, 'Behold, I will cause breath to enter you that you may come to life. I will put sinews on you, make flesh grow back on you, cover you with skin and put breath in you that you may come alive; and you will know that I am the LORD.'"
>
> verses 5–6

Prophecy calls forth the breath of God to enter difficult circumstances and situations. This "breath" is the Holy Spirit Himself being released. As His breath blows into the fragmented structures of people's lives, then families, churches, cities and nations can come together and live. God is the source of life, and prophecy acts as a refreshing wind that brings His life-giving oxygen to a stale and dry environment.

Breathe life, O God, into us, Your Church. Breathe upon the nations. Awaken us that we might truly know You.

So I Prophesied

Let's move to the next installment:

> So I prophesied as I was commanded; and as I prophesied, there was a noise, and behold, a rattling; and the bones came together, bone to its bone. And I looked, and behold, sinews were on

them, and flesh grew and skin covered them; but there was no breath in them.

Ezekiel 37:7–8

Who does the prophesying? We do. We just do it! Whatever God has called us to do, we are the ones who do it. The Holy Spirit does not fall on us and knock us down and pour things into us, and then push them out of us, by force. We begin by faith to speak out the small words we have received, and then God multiplies those words in our mouths. There are different levels of revelation, for sure. But you have to start somewhere.

Much of the time when I prophesy, I do not feel any special anointing or push from within; I just do it because I know God wants to speak. I yield my voice to Him and then I speak forth His word. We do not have to rely on some special feeling or manifestation to cause us to open our mouths. There is a sense in which we prophesy by faith. "Since we have gifts that differ according to the grace given to us, each of us is to exercise them accordingly: if prophecy, according to the proportion of his faith" (Romans 12:6). But please learn to stay in your measure of faith!

Nowhere in the Bible does it say the Holy Spirit speaks according to the gift of tongues. Nor does it say angels are to preach the everlasting Gospel for us. Guess what? Nowhere in the Bible does it say God prophesies, either. He gives the inspiration; we supply the perspiration. In other words, all vocal gifts are released through the vocal cords of a living being. All God is looking for is a donkey He can come and sit on who will carry Him into the city. Hey, I qualify for that! How about you?

Let Your breath enter my being, O Lord, and let me exhale words of life.

The word *command* means "to appoint" or "to be charged"— not so much by prompting but by commandment. This term denotes stewardship. Just as we are stewards of our money and give because God's Word tells us to, we are to be stewards of the word of the Lord. We should not act like children who have to be reminded continuously to do their daily chores. Maturity is doing what you are commanded without being told over and over to do it. Maturity and love emphasize obedience. Maturity is obeying even when you are not told to obey. "If anyone loves Me, he will keep My word; and My Father will love him, and We will come to him and make Our abode with him" (John 14:23).

As we begin to step out on that limb of faith called *r-i-s-k*, miraculous things happen. As Ezekiel stepped out and spoke to those dry bones, he heard a noise as those bones began rattling and moving together. Just imagine the word of the Lord coming through *you* and causing new life to spring up in a person or in a body of believers or even in a nation. It can happen!

When we step out in faith and do what we know to do, something happens. A noise begins to erupt from within people whose lives are being quickened by the word of the Lord. A rattling goes on in those dry bones as they come together, bone to bone, to form a structure for life. People get excited and start moving when prophecy touches their dry places and the wine begins to lift their spirits and they start to act like the people God created them to be. It is the noise of celebrating life. One thing I learned from the births of our four children—life brings a lot of noise to the house!

Another kind of noise, too, often follows prophetic revelation: the noise of persecution. People get unsettled when the status quo is disturbed. Jesus was a master at disturbing the status quo of religious people. And if we speak the testimony of Jesus, we will rattle the religious and they will make an awful noise. But praise God for those who dare to disturb religion and bring forth life.

Prophesy to the Breath

We see, next, God teaching Ezekiel prophetic intercession:

> Then He said to me, "Prophesy to the breath, prophesy, son of man, and say to the breath, 'Thus says the Lord GOD, "Come from the four winds, O breath, and breathe on these slain, that they come to life.""

> Ezekiel 37:9

God was instructing Ezekiel how to speak prophetic prayers, inviting the Spirit of God to bring life to the dead. Ezekiel was prophesying to the breath—to the wind!

If you do not think you know how to hear the word of the Lord and prophesy, just pick up your Bible and begin to declare the living Word over those whom you know to be dead. Anyone who can read can prophesy the Word of God. He has already told us what His will is, so declare it in prayer over those you know. Declare it over your families, your cities, your nation. Speak to the wind! Address the heavenlies and call for a new beginning to come forth. Declare life through the power of prophetic proclamation. Let life *be*, in Jesus' name.

Calling Forth the Army

Finally, we must prophesy out of God's bigger vision: "So I prophesied as He commanded me, and the breath came into them, and they came to life and stood on their feet, an exceedingly great army" (Ezekiel 37:10).

Let God fill your heart with a vision of His purposes. Out of the inspiration of Scripture and by the current daily operation of the revelatory inspiration of the Holy Spirit on our lives, we can declare that which is not as though it already is (see Romans 4:17). We can declare God's plan for our generation.

But you say, "I do not know a word for my city or my generation." Then prophesy one from another generation, as Daniel did. Daniel took a prophecy from Jeremiah 29, more than a generation before him, and prophesied those words to his own generation exiled in Babylon.

Study your family history or your city's history and find promises of God that will lift your family or city out of death into life. Apply yourself to the written Word of God, and inspiration will spring forth into your prayer life and convert your everyday place of living. Then you can go out into the streets and prophesy to the woman at the grocery store, the man at the service station and your next-door neighbor, speaking the living Word of God into their lives. You will watch an exceedingly great army begin to arise out of the throngs of death and take on the life of God. Do not wait for a revolution; *be* the revolution!

You do not know whom you will have an impact on. That one you speak to just might end up influencing the world. You might see dry bones, but look deeper into the heart of God. Prophesy life.

⟶ P R A Y E R ⟵

Holy God, I see dry bones, but I know they can live. I want to be one who prophesies life to others for edification, exhortation and comfort. I submit myself to You and ask for the baptism of fire to consecrate my life to You and Your will. I volunteer freely in the day of Your power, and I ask that You empower me with a fresh baptism from on high.

Fill my heart with a vision of Your purposes. Teach me to declare life wherever I go. Help me to look on the temporal, and then look up for the spiritual, and speak life to my valley of dry bones. Come, Holy Spirit, breathe on my life. Breathe on my family. Breathe on my church.

Breathe on my city and my nation. Bring life from the dead for the glory of King Jesus. Amen.

Embracing Your Calling—Day 20

1. What new insights did you gain from Ezekiel 37?

2. How can you declare life over your life, family, city and church?

3. Have you heard more prophetic words that judge and correct or that edify and comfort? What are the benefits of a culture that prophesies life?

4. Look at a situation in your life right now where the "bones are very dry." Apply what you have learned from this reading and begin to prophesy life to those "bones." Do not give up. Prophesy until you see life.

Paradigm Shifts for a Prophetic Lifestyle

As we have crossed the threshold of a new era in the Lord, there will be a lot of shifting taking place in the Church and the world. It is the time of completing unfinished business, a time of cleansing and a time to get prepared for a spiritual "Church-quake" to transpire in the life of what some prophetic voices call the "third-day Church." With this view in mind, let me present some thoughts on paradigm shifts for a prophetic lifestyle in the 21st century.

- An "apostolic relational mandate" is being released emphasizing networking rather than vertical authority structures. This fresh emphasis on cross-pollination will replace many of the inbred church associations, which are strife-ridden by the spirit of competition and control.
- While in worship I was given the following phases: "When the Apostolic is Made Personal (AMP) there will be Mighty Authority in the Prophetic (MAP) in that day. The Lord will amplify His voice in those relational renewal centers and the Holy Spirit will put them on His map."

- Confrontation shall come with the "political spirit." Even as the prophetic movement exposed and confronted the religious spirit in the Church, so an apostolic movement of grace and truth will expose and lay an ax at the historical root of the political spirit in the Church.

- The restoration of David's Tabernacle as prophesied in Amos 9:12 and Acts 15:16–18 shall escalate, resulting in authentic 24-hour houses of prayer and praise, worship and intercession sprinkled across the nations. New creative songs and sounds shall emerge as it was with the radical ministry of William and Katherine Booth's Salvation Army bands. Praise, once again, will not be confined to the "four walls of the church" but will spill out into the open-air arena.

- In the Church there will be a continued theological shift away from the false theory of cessationism (the belief that spiritual gifts passed away with the closing of the canon of Scripture or the second generation apostles of the early Church). In other words, cessationism is going to cease!

- A new signs and wonders movement is growing. Healing rooms and centers will be instituted in many cities devoted to praying for the sick and casting out evil spirits (see Luke 10). Parades of people healed of various diseases will once again occur as in the days of the life of John G. Lake in the 1920s.

- This move of God will be so powerful that the Church will gather in stadiums to worship—both the collective Church in given regions as well as some local congregations growing so large that they will fill stadiums for their celebration worship services.

- There is and will be a great move of the Holy Spirit among women. Many women will be released into the fivefold ministry and they will be used in worldwide revival and reformation, which is upon us. Ultimately, the issue will not primarily be doctrinal. It will be one of necessity due to the volume of need for laborers for the harvest. The coming period could easily be termed "The Era of Women Preachers."

- A renewed "quietist" movement will emerge as believers in Christ find the "secret place" of the Most High to truly be their dwelling place (see Psalm 91). A fresh revelation of intimacy with God, communion with their lover/husbandman and Master will come forth. A generation in the spirit of Mary of Bethany will arise and gladly "waste their lives" on the Lord.

- A fresh Holiness movement will spring up in the Church worldwide. Its emphasis shall be one of the Father's mercies mixed with an authentic spirit of conviction of sin (see John 16), causing many to repent and their stained garments to be experientially cleansed by the power and blood of the Lord Jesus Christ.

- The Body of Christ will awaken to her call and responsibility to reach and lift up the poor and oppressed as stated in Isaiah 58:7–12. Finances will be released to care for the widow and the orphan as declared in James 1:27. Chains of orphanages will come forth as the Church awakens from her self-centered lifestyles and hilarious, joyful giving is restored.

- We will see tremendous transfers of wealth into the Kingdom of God through the ministry of "marketplace" apostles and prophets. Those with anointing for business, administration and creativity shall be blessed—not resisted—by the Church. The wall between clergy/laity and secular marketplace/spiritual ministry shall come down.

- An extravagant youth movement is coming to the global Body of Christ that will "rock the nations." Public events will be led by youth to pray and fast for revival, which will spread rapidly around the nations. This will be a transgenerational anointing where the hearts of the fathers are turned to the children and the hearts of the children to the Father (see Malachi 4:5–6).

- A wave of "identificational repentance" will overwhelm a remnant of the Gentile Church causing her to repent of her historical wrongs against the Jewish people. In response to this, a revelation of the Sabbath rest shall be released from the throne of grace that will be non-legalistic and result in healing for many.

- It is the devil's strategy to precipitate another type of holocaust, but God will raise up trumpeters like Mordecai who shall prepare the corporate Esther (the Church) for such a time as this. Radical prayer will open a hedge of protection for the Jewish people as the shields of the earth belong to the Lord.

- A "convergence of the ages" shall come upon us. The anointings of Pentecostal fire, the healing and deliverance crusades, the Latter Rain presence, the evangelical burden for the lost, the charismatic gifts, the Jesus People zeal, the Third Wave credibility, the revelation of the prophetic movement and the relational networking of the apostolic reformation shall all merge together into a tidal wave that will be greater than the impact of the Reformation of five hundred years ago. This will ultimately create what could be called "the great transformation of the Church."

- Radical deeds of identificational repentance, acts of mercy to the poor and the oppressed, presence and power encounters to the sick and the demonized, warrior praise and intercession arising over cities will mount as a revolution comes upon the global Body of Christ and creates a great societal awakening! If history books are written of the years that lie ahead, they might be titled *The Days of His Glorious Presence*.

I am sure much more will occur as these days unfold. We see in part, know in part and prophesy in part. But when we each bring our own part to the table, it creates a whole. This is part of what I saw fourteen years ago and I still will declare it until we see it fully! This is part of what I perceive. The Holy Spirit will give other parts to other players as we cooperate together and the ATM—the "Apostolic Team Ministry"—comes forth.

I encourage you to keep these thoughts in front of you in the days ahead and ask the Holy Spirit how to walk these out in your own life. Prophetic revelation is a key to bringing forth an end-time army of believers who will take the Gospel to the four corners of the earth and spread the testimony of Jesus from pole to pole. Can you hear the call? Can you feel the Spirit moving on your heart for you to arise and take your place in the prophetic army God is forming? May we all join forces under the leadership of the Almighty, and move forward to meet our Bridegroom as He comes in the power of His might to claim His inheritance.

When You Have Done All

As I conclude today's reading and this book on the lifestyle of a prophet and those with prophetic giftings, I want to note one more paradigm shift. It actually is not as much a shift as it is a posture that believers in Christ have embraced for centuries, and today we, too, must embrace.

To do this I want to share a bit of my story for those of you who may not be aware of what has gone on behind the scenes. I trust it will encourage you on your journey as a prophetic person following the encouragement of Ephesians 6:13: "And having done everything . . . stand firm" (NASB).

I never once thought my life would go the direction it has over the last decade. Fifteen years ago I had no reason to fear having to face a disease such as cancer, particularly since I knew of no major history of it in my family. And yet since 2002 I have fought a grueling battle against non-Hodgkin's lymphoma. Prayer has always been my first weapon, though I have sought input and treatment along the way from as many sources as possible. I have endured dozens of treatments, had some amazing God encounters and have been pronounced clear and free of cancer at least three times—only to find it return in a different region of my body.

But to be completely transparent, I am not sure even my own bout with cancer could prepare me for the degree of loss I have faced in almost every area of life and ministry in recent years.

Suffering Times Two

Shortly after I began fighting for my own life, my dear wife of 32 years, Michal Ann Goll, discovered she had colon cancer. After having her entire colon removed one Christmas, we had great hopes of her conquering this beast and we were believing the Lord for new body parts. She was relentless in her pursuit of healing and wholeness and, in my opinion, fought harder than I ever did. Yet her cancer continued to spread to several other organ systems.

Despite this, Michal Ann never lost her smile, she never let one negative word be echoed in her midst and she loved God through every moment. She was devoted to the Word of God, lived a hidden life of prayer and was fearless in the face of the enemy.

Together we fought hard. We prayed, fasted, declared Scripture, praised the Lord, took communion, were committed to the local church, were properly aligned with apostolic authority, continued to believe in the supernatural . . . and on and on. We'd experienced miracles several times before and had seen every gift of the Holy Spirit flow through our own lives into the lives of others around the world. We were desperate and did everything we knew to come out on the other side victorious.

We made sure to identify and shut every generational door that might have been jarred even a little bit.

And yet the battle raged on.

We took an integrated approach the entire time—and I still do to this day. We brought together the best of many healing streams. We received counsel from the best and intensive prayer from those who move extraordinarily in the gifts of healings and working of miracles today. We combined the very best of alternative and traditional medicine with nutritional understandings, soaking worship and high praise. We had hands laid on us by the elders of the city, were interceded for by the global prayer movement and extended forgiveness wherever needed.

And yet the battle raged on.

We were faithful in our marriage covenant and faithful to the Lord. I'm not saying we were perfect. I am not perfect. I stand by grace in faith in the finished work of Calvary, as every believer does. But I do know Michal Ann and I did everything we could, and we trusted in God to do what we could not.

And yet the battle raged on.

The result of our fight? On September 15, 2008, after four years of warring against cancer, my dear wife moved on to a great eternal realm called heaven. Thank God for heaven! We are only separated for a short time. Still, it is perplexing to say the least why I made it and she did not. Michal Ann was an amazing champion for the Lord. My kids and I greatly miss her to this day.

Adding Salt to My Wounds

Losing my wife was hard enough. Yet in the midst of my grieving—and while still fighting my own battle with cancer—I received another blow. Financial hits to both my personal and ministerial life left me almost drained. Within a short time, I lost three-fourths of my monthly donor base funding our global ministry. Due to medical expenses not covered by insurance and other unforeseen complications, I ended up with a massive amount of accumulated debt. Prior to this, I had paid every bill on time and had a great credit history.

As the bills piled up, my fight against cancer continued as I used every means possible to win. On October 7, 2009, I finally received news that the 3½-by-2½-inch cancerous growth close to my stomach had melted and that every cancer cell advancing in my body was eradicated. Praise the Lord! I thank God for my second chance in life and declare that the cancer will not return again.

But then I faced the reality that I am a single parent struggling to stay afloat. My four miracle kids were left with no grandparents, no mom and a dad fighting for his very existence. Although that may sound extreme, it is not only the truth, it is merely the tip of the iceberg of what has occurred in my life during the past fifteen years.

I am not alone in my journey. Some of you have been there as well. We have been enduring seasons of storms. And for many of us, these seasons have ushered us into times of severe questioning.

The Questions Come

What did I do to deserve all of this? This was one of the most prominent thoughts ringing in my head during the storms of this last decade. After all, I'd walked with the Lord every day of life since youth. Jesus has been my closest friend and companion through all my 58 years (I just celebrated my sixtieth birthday at the writing of this book). I had been in full-time vocational ministry since I graduated from college in 1974. I had been true to the light given me and never backed away from the progressive truths as an ambassador of Christ. Why me? Why my family?

At times I felt like Job. I became acquainted with some of his well-meaning friends, each of whom gave me frequent input on the reasons why we were incurring such difficulties. It was supposedly because we prayed wrongly against some power of darkness or didn't have enough faith. Some chided that I must have been ignorant of God's Word concerning healing, while others reasoned that we were encountering such difficulties because we took a stand for Israel. Still others said it was because we had hidden sin, and if we would only bring it to the light the circumstances would end. A few acquaintances even claimed my suffering was because I wasn't a vegan.

People gave us every lotion, potion and natural remedy under the sun. I finally had to come to the conclusion that they cared for us and merely wanted us fixed. Yet the truth was, I wanted our situation fixed more than they did. As a result, I had to learn to love these well-meaning people while maintaining my personal convictions and my consecration and devotion to Jesus. The culmination of my trials and others' unsolicited input gave me the opportunity to trust the Lord with all my heart and lean not on my own understanding (see Proverbs 3:5).

Lessons Learned

If I had to do it all over again, there is little I would change in the approach Michal Ann and I took. Of all things, I would have sat more on my southern front porch with my Annie, quietly drinking green tea in our rocking chairs, enjoying God and nature. Just being. Resting. Enjoying. I learned from my oncologist that every day we have is a gift from God.

And so I am left with today—for which I am truly grateful. I do not take it for granted, nor do I want to ignore the pain endured through these past storms. I am yet a work in progress. I'm still leaning in upon my beloved Jesus and learning more each day. But I know I can at least share with you some basic practical concepts that have been anchors in my life along the way. Here are a few.

1. God is good—all the time! This is at the top of my list on purpose. I believe and declare loudly, "The LORD is good to all, and His tender mercies are over all His works" (Psalm 145:9, NKJV). If you want to be an overcomer in any area of life, you must have this foundational truth in place. Everything else hinges on this one truth. Always remember, Jesus "went about doing good and healing all who were oppressed by the devil" (Acts 10:38). He is "the same yesterday and today and forever," and He is always going about doing good (Hebrews 13:8).

2. All things work together for good. I hang my hat on this belief system. Romans 8:28 uncompromisingly declares: "And we know that all things work together for good to those who love God, to those who are called according to His purpose." That verse is not for some generic person "out there"; it is for me and for you! Note that the verse does not say "everything is good" or that "God causes everything." Yet somehow in the great majesty of who He is, God takes even our failures, temporary disappointments and messed-up circumstances, and, when we are yielded to Him, He reconfigures them to work together for good. That is the Jesus I know dearly.

3. Keep your expectations high. Just because I have not seen every person get healed does not mean I will stop praying for the sick. I will not stop declaring the Good News of the Gospel of the Kingdom just because not everyone will be saved. Do not doubt in times of darkness what has been revealed in the light. Do not lower your theological bar to match temporary setbacks. Press on. Keep your expectations high and on God. Keep on believing.

4. Rely on a trusted community of believers. I am so grateful for the Body of Christ. Some have walked with my family and me through our dark night of the soul. I need God, and I also need you. The second part of 1 John 5:4 says: "And this is the victory that overcomes the world—our faith." It does not say "my faith"; it says "our faith." We need each other. Sometimes we just need the Body of Christ—Jesus with flesh on. Be a committed part of the community of believers called the Church.

5. *Be open to change.* This has probably been one of the hardest lessons for me during the last decade. I love consistency and stability. But to make it through to the other side you have to be flexible in the hands of the Master Potter. You must learn to recalibrate, adjust and understand that change is not your enemy; it is good. To help cut my monthly budget, two years ago I had to move out of my ministry center and into a set of small offices. I am now taking steps to make even more cuts. I have definitely felt the pruning of the Lord. I do not like it, but I know it is good. The truth is, whether we embrace it or not, things will change. To transition more smoothly, we must be open to new things, new revelations, new places and even new connections.

6. *Fear not!* Renounce fear—be delivered from it. Get whatever cleansing is needed, because what you fear will come upon you. Fear is not your friend. Fear is the opposite of faith. Fear paralyzes you, while faith propels you. Doubt your doubts and trust your dreams. Fear not! He is with you, beside you and in you. And as 1 John 4:4 says, "He who is in you is greater than he who is in the world."

7. *Never, never, never, never give up.* I carry a greeting card in my Bible. On the front it reads, "Never, never, never, never give up." And on the inside are these words: "I will never, never, never, never quit cheering for you." These were my dear wife's last words to me and our four kids. It was her last prophetic statement to the Body of Christ. Jesus is our dread champion! As you press on in life, put your hand to the plow and do not

look over your shoulder (see Luke 9:62). Keep looking straight ahead. God is not finished with you yet. He who began a good work in you will complete it (see Philippians 1:6).

8. You are not a victim; you are a victor! We must engraft this truth into our souls. At one of my low points, one of my kids lovingly got in my face and said something like, "Dad, you've got to rise above this. Trauma happens in life, but you must not be its victim." I am here to tell you I am a victor in Christ Jesus, and so are you! Jesus always leads us into a triumphant processional: "But thanks be to God, who always leads us in triumph in Christ, and manifests through us the sweet aroma of the knowledge of Him in every place" (2 Corinthians 2:14). You are not a victim; you are more than a conqueror in Christ Jesus.

Let me reemphasize, I am still a work in progress. My journey—pain and all—is still being walked out. But I pray that you can benefit from the lessons I am learning in the process of becoming. I have lived an amazing life and am so grateful that I have been given a second chance in life. I pray that whatever season of life you are in, you will cling as I have to the truth of Ephesians 6:10: "Finally, be strong in the Lord and in the strength of His might." And when you have done all . . . stand.

Might I add something else? The best is yet to come. Yes, you heard me. I am a product of grace—and by grace, the best is yet to come!

You Are His Workmanship

Ephesians 2:10 boldly declares that "we are His workmanship, created in Christ Jesus for good works, which God prepared beforehand so that we would walk in them." The purpose of a lifestyle—not just inconsistent occasions—of intimacy, wisdom and revelation is so that we can walk in all that "God prepared beforehand." What a glorious privilege God has extended to us!

Well, we have finished 21 days of embracing your calling. Have you more fully embraced that to which you have been called? Remember, some see dry bones, but I see an army! What you behold you become. I am still in the process of becoming. Yes, by grace, I am becoming more like Jesus every day. How about you?

Is that not what the lifestyle of a true prophet and a prophetic community is ultimately about? As for me and my house, we will draw near to God as He has and does draw near to us. It is time for all gifts, fruit and wisdom to come into agreement. That is what I'm laboring for.

⟹ PRAYER ⟸

Thank You, my precious Lord and Savior, for calling me out of darkness into Your marvelous light. You see me, You love me deeply and You draw me to Yourself. I am so grateful for life—life abiding in You, walking with You, learning with You, co-laboring together to see Your Kingdom come on earth as it is in heaven.

Draw me into a deeper lifestyle of intimacy; make me wise beyond my years and open the eyes of my heart to see You and what You see in this world. I ask for a fresh baptism of Your Spirit to cleanse and empower me for the work of Your service. Come alive in me afresh and equip me to bear fruit for Your name's sake. I love You, Jesus. I commit my life into Your mighty hands.

Now to Him who is able to keep [me] from stumbling, and to make [me] stand in the presence of His glory blameless with great joy, to the only God our Savior, through Jesus Christ our

Lord, be glory, majesty, dominion and authority, before all time and now and forever. Amen.

Jude 1:24–25

▓ Embracing Your Calling—Day 21

1. Which paradigm shifts for the 21st century most resonate with you? Why?

2. What part of James's "When You Have Done All" story most impacted you? How could you relate?

3. Which of the eight lessons do you most want to embrace? Why?

4. Before you finish this book, review the "Embracing Your Calling" sections throughout the book, specifically the last action step. Take time to pray and then put feet to your prayers—take the necessary steps to incorporate into your daily life what you have learned and heard from the Lord. Make it a part of your lifestyle, and may Jesus be glorified.

Notes

Reading for Day 3: Coming into the Light

1. Ed Silvoso, *That None Should Perish* (Ventura, Calif.: Regal, 1994), 154.

Reading for Day 4: Character to Carry the Gift

1. Leonard Ravenhill, quoted in T. Austin Sparks, *Prophetic Ministry* (Shippensburg, Pa.: Destiny Image, 2000), vii.
2. Sparks, *Prophetic*, 7–8.
3. Bill Hamon, *Prophets, Pitfalls and Principles* (Shippensburg, Pa.: Destiny Image, 1991), 9–10.

Reading for Day 6: Lovers of the Cross

1. Sparks, *Prophetic*, 53–54.
2. Rick Joyner, *Prophetic Ministry* (Charlotte, N.C.: MorningStar, 1997), 28.
3. Bill Hamon, *Prophets,* 21.
4. John and Paula Sandford, *The Elijah Task: A Call to Today's Prophets* (Tulsa: Victory House, 1979), 29.
5. Ed Dufresne, *The Prophet: Friend of God* (Temecula, Calif.: Ed Dufresne Ministries, 1989), 42–43.
6. Michael Brown, *Revolution in the Church* (Grand Rapids: Chosen, 2002), 224.

Reading for Day 9: Our Revelatory Storehouse

1. Kenneth Hagin, *Gifts of the Spirit* (Tulsa: Faith Library Publications, 1999), 53.
2. Dick Iverson, *The Holy Spirit Today* (Portland: Bible Temple, 1976), 155.

3. Derek Prince, "The Gift of Prophecy," *Teaching Tapes* (Ft. Lauderdale: Derek Prince Ministries, n.d.).
4. Ernest Gentile, *Your Sons & Daughters Shall Prophesy* (Grand Rapids: Chosen, 1999), 162.
5. Hamon, *Prophets*, 196–197.
6. C. Peter Wagner, *Your Spiritual Gifts Can Help Your Church Grow* (Ventura, Calif.: Regal, 1994), 200.

Reading for Day 10: Prophetic Ways of Wisdom

1. Michael Sullivant, *Prophetic Etiquette* (Lake Mary, Fla.: Creation House, 2000), 131–132.
2. Adapted from James W. Goll, "Equipping the Saints," *Vineyard* (Fall 1989).
3. Paraphrased from Derek Prince, "How to Judge Prophecy" (Charlotte, N.C.: Derek Prince Ministries, 1971).

Reading for Day 14: Avoiding the Snares

1. Joyner, *Prophetic*, 103.

Reading for Day 17: Unity in Diversity

1. Tommy Tenney, *God's Dream Team* (Ventura, Calif.: Regal, 1999), 19.
2. Cindy Jacobs, *The Voice of God* (Ventura, Calif.: Regal, 1995), 157–158.
3. Fuchsia Pickett, quoted in Kelly Varner, *The Three Prejudices* (Shippensburg, Pa.: Destiny Image, 1997), 31.
4. Edith Blumhofer, quoted in Sheri R. Benvenuti, "Pentecostal Women in Ministry: Where Do We Go from Here?," *Cyberjournal for Pentecostal-Charismatic Research* 1 (January 1997), http://www.pctii.org/cyberj/cyberj1/ben.html.
5. James W. Goll, *Father Forgive Us!* (Shippensburg, Pa.: Destiny Image, 1999), 109.

Reading for Day 18: Seizing Your Prophetic Destiny

1. This section was inspired by the writing and teaching of William Greenman. See his *How to Find Your Purpose in Life* (Pittsburgh: Whitaker, 1987), 163–176.
2. Kenneth W. Osbeck, *101 More Hymn Stories* (Grand Rapids: Kregel, 1985), 44.

Reading for Day 19: Growing in Revelation

1. See my study guides *War in the Heavenlies* and *Strategies of Intercession* for more on this subject.
2. See my study guide *Releasing Spiritual Gifts* for more on this subject.
3. See "The Power of Proclamation" in my study guide *Compassionate Prophetic Intercession* for more on this subject.
4. See my study guide *Experiencing Dreams and Visions* for more on this subject.
5. Graham Cooke, *Developing Your Prophetic Gifting* (Kent, Sussex, U.K.: Sovereign World, 1994), 145.
6. Derek Prince, "How to Judge Prophecy: Part 1," *New Wine* (January 1977): 15.

Reading for Day 20: Prophesy Life!

1. The inspiration for this section of the book came as I listened to a piercing yet humorous message by Larry Randolph, an author and prophetic minister of many years from Franklin, Tennessee. His message was entitled "The Anatomy of a Prophetic Word." He is the author of the book *User-Friendly Prophecy* (Destiny Image, 1998).

General Index

Scripture Index

Genesis

2:7 28
2:24–25 30
3:1–3 31
3:4–7 32
3:5 42
3:8 126
3:9 34
3:10 32
20:7 68
37:3–4 95
37:6–7 92
37:8 95
39:6 93
39:23 93
40:8 96, 127
41:15–16 96
41:39 98
41:41 94
45:7 94
50:19–21 97
50:20 94

Exodus

3:4 126
15:20 205
33:15–16 55
33:16 61

Numbers

11:25 120
11:26 120
11:29 52
12:6 148

Deuteronomy

13:1–5 119
18:20–22 119
30:19 215
34:9 84

Joshua

1:6–7, 9 228

Judges

4 206
4:4 205
16:1 160
16:4 161
16:7 161
16:15 162
16:16 162
16:17 162
16:19 162
16:20 162

16:22 163
16:25 164
16:28 164
21:25 191, 197

1 Samuel

3:1–14 80
3:3–4 54
3:9, 20 80
15:26–28 226
16 133
16:7 55
19:20 82
25 206

2 Samuel

5:23–25 126
7:2–5 132

1 Kings

16:31 65
18:4, 19 65
18:41 131
19:1–4 65
19:15–21 84
19:19–21 80

Scripture Index

James W. Goll is the director of Encounters Network, based in Franklin, Tennessee, dedicated to changing lives and impacting nations by releasing God's presence through the prophetic, intercessory and compassion ministry. James is also the international director of Prayer Storm, a 24/7 media-based prayer ministry. He is also founder of God Encounters Training—E-School of the Heart. James has his B.S. in Social Work from Missouri State University and his doctorate in Practical Ministry from the Wagner Leadership Institute.

After pastoring in the Midwest, James was thrust into the role of itinerant ministry around the globe. He has traveled extensively across every continent carrying a passion for Jesus wherever he goes. James desires to see the Body of Christ come into maturity and become the house of prayer for all nations. He is the author of numerous books and training manuals as well as a contributing writer for several periodicals.

James is a founding instructor in the Wagner Leadership Institute and the Christian Leadership University. He is a member of the Harvest International Ministry Apostolic Team and a consultant to several regional, national and international ministries. James and Michal Ann Goll were married for over 32 years before her graduation to heaven in the fall of 2008. Their four adult children all love Jesus. James continues to make his home in the beautiful rolling hills of Franklin, Tennessee.

For More Information:

James W. Goll
Encounters Network
P.O. Box 1653
Franklin, TN 37065
office phone: 615-599-5552
email: info@EncountersNetwork.com, or
info@PrayerStorm.com
websites: www.EncountersNetwork.com
www.PrayerStorm.com
www.JamesGoll.com
www.ENMedia.org
www.CompassionActs.com
www.GETeschool.com
www.IsraelPrayerCoalition.com
www.WomenontheFrontlines.com

Additional Resource Materials by James W. and Michal Ann Goll

The Lost Art of Intercession

God Encounters

Women on the Front Lines Series (with Michal Ann Goll)

Intercession

The Lost Art of Practicing His Presence

Praying for Israel's Destiny

The Coming Israel Awakening

The Beginner's Guide to Hearing God

The Coming Prophetic Revolution

The Call of the Elijah Revolution (with Lou Engle)

The Prophetic Intercessor

Shifting Shadows of Supernatural Experiences (with Julia Loren)

The Seer, expanded

The Seer 40 Day Devotional Journal

Prayer Storm

Prayer Storm Study Guide

The 365 Day Personal Prayer Guide

Empowered Prayer

Dream Language (with Michal Ann Goll)

Angelic Encounters (with Michal Ann Goll)

Discovering the Seer in You

Exploring the Nature and Gift of Dreams

Empowered Women (contributor)

God's Supernatural Power in You (contributor)

Adventures in the Prophetic (contributor)

The Beginner's Guide to Signs, Wonders and the Supernatural Life

The Reformer's Pledge (contributor)

Deliverance from Darkness

Deliverance from Darkness Study Guide

Exploring Dreams and Visions

Prayer Changes Things (contributor)

The Lost Art of Pure Worship (contributor)

Living the Supernatural Life

Over twenty additional study guides

Numerous CD, MP3 and DVD albums

More Life-Changing Insight from James W. Goll

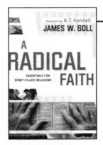

More from James W. Goll

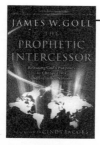

By offering you the secret to moving heaven and earth, James Goll will help you experience a whole new level of effectiveness in personal, corporate and even international concerns. Don't wait—transform your prayer life today. Includes a practical 21-day devotional.

The Prophetic Intercessor

Many believe we are witnessing the beginning of the biblically foretold restoration of the Church and Israel. Get an inside glimpse at God's plans for the Jewish people and the Church's role in this prophetic look at the coming days.

The Coming Israel Awakening

Your prayers affect God's prophetic timeline! Help usher in the time of Jesus' coming by praying for a key appointment on God's prophetic calendar: the restoration of Israel. James Goll shares the models of prayer for this crucial nation in God's plans. Join with intercessors worldwide to pray for Israel—and watch as God fulfills His promises through her.

Praying for Israel's Destiny